An Independent People

The Way We Lived in North Carolina, 1770–1820

© 1983 The University of North
Carolina Press

Manufactured in the United States
of America

*Library of Congress Cataloging in
Publication Data*

Watson, Harry L.
   An independent people.

   Bibliography: p.
   1. North Carolina—History—1775–
1865.   2. North Carolina—History—
Revolution, 1775–1783.   3. North
Carolina—Social life and customs.
4. North Carolina—Description and
travel—1981–   —Guide-books.
   5. Historic sites—North Carolina—
Guide-books.   I. Nathans, Sydney.
   II. North Carolina. Dept. of Cultural
Resources. III. Title.
F258.W37 1983   975.6′03   82-20098
ISBN 0-8078-1550-0
ISBN 0-8078-4102-1 (pbk.)

An Independent People

The Way We Lived in North Carolina, 1770–1820

Published for the North Carolina Department of Cultural Resources

by The University of North Carolina Press   *Chapel Hill*

Editor:
Sydney Nathans

Consultants:
Larry Misenheimer
William S. Price, Jr.

This publication has been made possible through a grant from the National Endowment for the Humanities.

The Way We Lived series was developed under the guidance of the Historic Sites Section, Division of Archives and History, North Carolina Department of Cultural Resources.

(Title page) The John Haley House (1786), High Point Museum, Guilford County. Few houses in the entire colony were brick. The Haleys brought this building tradition from Pennsylvania.

(Right) Interior of the Haley House.

Christine Alexander took the photographs not otherwise credited in this book.

Text by Harry L. Watson

Research and Marginalia by Jean B. Anderson

Design and Art Editing by Christine Alexander

Winkler's Bakery (1800), Old Salem, Forsyth County. The Salem Diary for 11 May 1813 noted that "Because of the considerable advance in the price of wheat Br. Winkler has found it necessary to reduce the weight of a loaf of bread." Fries, ed., *Records of the Moravians*, vol. 7.

Experiencing History

This series of books, *The Way We Lived*, is based on the premise that the past can be most fully comprehended through the combined impact of two experiences: reading history and visiting historic places. The text of this volume (the second in a series of five) is therefore coordinated with a variety of historical sites. Most places pictured as well as those mentioned in the margins are open to the public regularly or by appointment. Information about visiting and exact locations may be obtained locally.

Our objective in specifying sites has not been to compile a complete or comprehensive catalogue of historic places in the state; rather it has been to guide the reader to a representative selection of sites that exemplify the major themes of the text.

Many excellent examples that might have served our purpose equally well have been omitted. Others now in the planning or working stages of restoration may be expected to swell the number of unnamed sites. We can only leave to the readers the pleasure of their discovery and the hope that this volume will serve as a stimulus to further reading and exploration.

Contents

Overview

In 1770 North Carolina sheltered a remarkable human diversity. Parts of the Albemarle Sound region had been settled by the English for more than a century. There and along the lower reaches of the Cape Fear River wealthy farmers and their Afro-American slaves had laid the basis for a plantation society. In the western mountains, Cherokee Indians continued their traditional ways of life with little or no interference from distant whites. In between, English, Scotch-Irish, German, and Highland Scottish settlers carved out new homes in the dense forest. The inhabitants of the largest towns differed markedly from their rural neighbors in their work, their social position, and their personal opportunity. The people of North Carolina were not clearly united in politics, language, religion, or any other cultural characteristics. In many ways it would be difficult to think of them as members of the same society.

If North Carolinians shared any characteristic besides diversity, it was their basic reliance on the outside world for a variety of cultural and commercial necessities. For the most part, Carolinians supplied themselves with the corn, meat, shelter, and clothing that were necessary for simple survival, but their self-sufficiency was more a condition of wilderness isolation than true independence. Sophisticated products and ideas almost always came from elsewhere. Iron, salt, and rum came from the schooners that docked at New Bern, Edenton, and Wilmington. Fashions, furniture, and elaborate building designs came from sketches published in Europe. Religious authority came from clergymen born and trained abroad, and governmental power came from Great Britain in the person of a royal governor.

By 1820 North Carolina's diversity and dependency had begun to change. A common language and economy prevailed among most of the children of the white pioneers, regardless of their parents' ethnic origins. Assorted African tribesmen suffered a more painful process of assimilation with each other in the rigors of slavery. Considerable economic dependency on outsiders persisted, but activist citizens were pushing hard for reforms to remedy this condition. Waves of religious revivalism had brought a fundamental shift in popular worship. Most importantly, North Carolina had fought and won a war for political independence and had joined the federal Union. Remnants of the older state of affairs persisted, but nineteenth-century North Carolina had become an independent society.

The changes had come about as part of an economic and political transformation. The first generation of pioneers had adopted a self-

Farming tools, 1790. Limited to heavy iron or wooden implements, these were exhausting to use. Shown are the plow and its attachments, sickle, scythe, flail, rake, and fork.

Smyth made some interesting observations: "Almost every man in this country has been the fabricator of his own fortune, and many of them are very opulent. Some have obtained their riches by commerce, others by the practice of law, which in this province is peculiarly lucrative, and extremely oppressive; but most have acquired their possessions by cropping farming, and industry."

sufficient life-style as a necessity for survival. They built their homes from logs, fed their livestock from the forest floor, raised their own supplies of food and fiber, and sold a tiny surplus to obtain what they could not make themselves. Gradually this life-style had begun to give way to the widening world of the market economy. Farmers had raised more and more crops for sale and purchased increased supplies from the stores they found in growing towns and villages. As years passed and civilization developed, farmers sought ways to obtain more store-bought goods without sacrificing the cherished independence of the self-sufficient freeholders.

The secret to successful commercial farming was labor, for the farmer who commanded the most laborers could raise the greatest surplus. Beyond the members of the farmer's family, almost all available workers were slaves; the institution of slavery consequently grew and strengthened as expanding farms became plantations. Formidable geographical handicaps drove up freight rates for exported plantation products and thus kept North Carolina's planters less prosperous than their counterparts elsewhere, but they did their best to establish the polished and genteel world of a leisured aristocracy. Bolstered by their property, education, and personal connections, the planters joined with merchants, lawyers, and other urban leaders to dominate public affairs of the colony and later the state.

North Carolina's elite did not emerge without challenge. Slaves resisted their masters' power in a variety of ways both overt and covert. In the late 1760s, moreover, a movement of western farmers who called themselves Regulators violently protested the undemocratic features of North Carolina's economic and political order. Commanded by royal governor William Tryon, eastern militiamen crushed the Regulators in 1771 at the Battle of Alamance. During the American Revolution, westerners and smaller farmers pushed for a more democratic political system, but they achieved only limited success. For the most part, yeomen who could not match the resources of the largest slaveholders either kept silent or did their best to imitate the gentry. As they did so, society in North Carolina gradually shifted from the frontier stage and took on the contours of the antebellum South.

During this long-term process of social transformation, other developments brought North Carolina through a political revolution. British leaders sought to tax the colonies and to reduce them more directly to imperial control. These efforts sparked a bitter resistance because the colonists' intellectual heritage and their way of life had bred in them a fierce love of individual and collective liberty.

As they won their political independence, free North Carolinians sought to define the character of their new republic. Some gentlemen among the educated elite relied on human reason and the historical lessons of ancient republics as sufficient guides for the young state

Colonial farmer using sickle.

and its rulers. Less prominent Carolinians seemed more cautious and hearkened to Protestant evangelists who taught that personal and national salvation would only come through faith in the word of God. Less speculative political thinkers warned that new technology and improvements in transportation were vital to the state's prosperity, regardless of its ideological or theological preferences. The debate over republicanism was far from over when the second decade of the nineteenth century ended, but all parties in the discussion still appealed to the ideal of personal independence for white freemen, in an unchanging society based on slavery and agriculture.

As they moved through half a century of social and political change, North Carolinians left signs of their steady transformation in the buildings and other material products of their culture. Log cabins gave way to frame cottages, and changing private homes revealed a shift in ideal family arrangements. Architectural fashions from distant capitals translated themselves into appropriate forms for Carolina farmhouses. Cultural monuments like schools, churches, and public buildings displayed the tastes and ideals of an independent people.

Changes in politics, economics, religion, and ideology had an impact on Carolina life-styles, just as the daily lives of the people exerted a pervasive pressure on the direction of larger historical events. Visitors to North Carolina's historic sites can witness the history of an era as they follow the physical evolution of the way we lived.

4

The Forest, the Indians, and the Yeoman Family

In the winter of 1783–84, German traveler Johann David Schöpf made a trip through the former British colony of North Carolina. In the account he later published, Schöpf searched for an image to convey his first impressions of the newly independent state. "The country . . . must be imagined as a continuous measureless forest," he began, "an ocean of trees in which only here and there cultivated spots, what are called plantations . . . are to be seen." A decade earlier, a British army officer had had a similar reaction. J. F. D. Smyth recalled "an universal gloomy shade, rendered dismal by the intermixing branches of the lofty trees, which overspread the whole country, and [which] the sun never pervades." Another voyager reported that "the mariners, going upon the coast in spring, have smelt the pines when several leagues at sea." Ebenezer Hazard, a Philadelphian, spoke more matter-of-factly. "The Country is a Pine Barren," he noted in his diary. "I have frequently rode 5 & 6 miles in this Journey without seeing any Sign of Cultivation."

When they agreed on little else, travelers to North Carolina in the 1770s and 1780s concurred about the forest. Trees were everywhere: tangled oaks and cypresses where the ground was swampy in the east, stately pines where it was dry. To the west, oaks, hickories, walnuts, chestnuts, poplars, and an astonishing variety of other species took over, but always there were woods—dark, forbidding, and dense. By 1770 permanent European settlers had lived in this environment for over a hundred years, but still the wilderness felt very close. Whatever the people of North Carolina accomplished in the name of civilization—the houses they built, the fields they cleared and planted, the towns they made by the riverbanks—all took shape against a backdrop of seemingly endless forest.

The Joyce Kilmer Memorial Forest, in Graham County, is one of the very few patches of completely virgin timberland still remaining in the state today. Nourished by especially high rainfall in the area, trees in this 3,500-acre tract have grown to immense proportions. The tulip poplars are especially impressive, but other hardwoods and hemlocks are prevalent as well. The forests that dominated the eastern North Carolina landscape in the eighteenth century consisted of thick and lofty long-leafed pines, widely spaced and bare of branches for as many as fifty feet up the trunk. Dense shade and occasional brushfires eliminated undergrowth, so the traveler could see for a mile or more beneath the deep canopy of needled branches. Some observers claimed that the forest floor was so clear and flat that a

(Opposite and below) Joyce Kilmer Memorial Forest, Nantahala National Forest, Graham County.

Weymouth Woods Sandhills Nature Preserve, Southern Pines, Moore County, contains stands of virgin long-leaf pines, while Merchants Millpond State Park, Gates County, shows the swamplands with their huge cypress trees and impenetrable terrain of northeastern North Carolina.

Ebenezer Hazard wrote a memo to himself in his diary after a hard lesson: "Take no more short cuts in North Carolina—Had to cross two Mill Dams & met with great Difficulty. Rode through a very gloomy Cypress Swamp:—lost my way—."

Major John A. Lillington's childhood diary reflects his life in 1800, with a widowed mother involved in the turpentine industry and an irritating little sister: "Nov. 11—Mama is gone to the Tarkiln agin today and lift Sarah ann and myself to keep house I have been seeing the cotton put away and that is all I can say this morning. I have been draoring landskips and ladys and if I had some paint I would paint them. Nov. 19—Mama is gone to the Tarkiln and that is all I can say for nothing at all happens. Nov. 26—We have not seen anybody at all this fournoon. . . . Sarahann is a very bad Girl today."

coach and four horses could travel off the road in any direction, for an indefinite distance. The steep terrain and tangled growth of the Appalachian forest creates a different effect, but the visitor in Joyce Kilmer can sense more fully than elsewhere the overpowering presence of the wilderness described by Schöpf, Smyth, and Hazard.

To a large extent, the people of North Carolina made a living from the trees around them. Pines were scarred with V-shaped notches and basins were hacked in each trunk to catch the flowing sap. When collected and poured into barrels, the sap sold well as turpentine or, when distilled, as spirits of turpentine. These pines eventually died, and when the split lengths of fallen lightwood were baked in earthen ovens, black tar oozed into holes scooped out for the purpose. Tar that was boiled or burned left a residue called "pitch," an even more valuable substance. Tar, pitch, and turpentine were called "naval stores" and they found a ready market as waterproofing materials in an age of wooden sailing vessels. Water-driven sawmills also cut pine logs into planks, while oak and cypress trees were the raw materials for vast quantities of handmade barrel staves and shingles. Skilled coopers fashioned barrels from many of these staves to hold the naval stores, while large cargoes of other staves were exported.

Cooper's shop, Single Brothers' House, Old Salem, Forsyth County. Courtesy Old Salem Restoration.

Lumber and naval stores were generally floated to market on rafts and flatboats, but many North Carolinians lived too far from navigable water to make this practice feasible. These settlers exploited the forest by raising livestock, a product that carried itself to market. Cattle and hogs wandered freely in the woods and fed on nuts, roots, cane, reeds, and Spanish moss. In the fall roundup, every farmer identified his stock by the slits he had made in the animals' ears. After marking the yearlings, the backcountry herdsman drove the increase of his stock to town. His market might be located in North Carolina, but it could just as easily be Charleston, Norfolk, or even Philadelphia. At the port, the animals were sometimes fattened with grain, then slaughtered and pickled in brine, packed into huge oak casks, and rolled into the hold of an oceangoing vessel. Like lumber and naval stores, beef and pork were forest-grown commodities that were crucial to export commerce and made the fortune of many an urbane merchant and courtly planter.

Passing travelers noted the economic importance of the forest eventually, but at first sight it was the scattered tiny fields and not the efficient use of forest resources that reminded observers of the presence of civilization. In the 1770s tobacco was still mostly confined to the strip of northern counties near Virginia, while rice and indigo appeared on the lower Cape Fear River. Rice had been introduced from South Carolina; indigo was the source of a dark blue dye very popular in Britain. Cotton, a staple of the nineteenth century, did not spread widely before the invention of Eli Whitney's gin in the 1790s. The most significant crop was corn, which the settlers ate themselves, fed to some of their animals, and marketed for gain. Wheat and flour were likewise important articles of trade and, like most of North Carolina's products, found their way eventually to the West Indies. These islands had been stripped of trees long before and every foot of arable land was turned to the cultivation of sugarcane. Many of the slaves who tilled the cane fields lived on North Carolina corn, pork, and beef; slept in barracks made of North Carolina lumber and shingles; and packed the sugar, molasses, and rum into barrels made from North Carolina staves. Of the products that were carried to Britain itself, naval stores and indigo received a government subsidy or "bounty." Remote as it sometimes seemed, the thinly settled colony was an integral unit in the British Empire.

Whether they took their living from the forest or from the fields (and most North Carolinians did some of both), a constant factor in the lives of eighteenth-century inhabitants was the importance of the land and its bounty. The shape of the terrain, the nature of the soil, the conditions of the weather—all had more direct influence on the pattern of human life than later generations would experience. The pervasive influence of the natural environment gave North Carolinians a common ground that divergent social arrangements could

Smyth told his countrymen: "Throughout the middle and back settlements of America, there is no other criterion to ascertain the property of black cattle, sheep, and hogs, but earmarks alone; and of horses, than brands with red hot irons, and earmarks also. Each person's mark differs from another; and they are all severally recorded by the clerk of the county courts wherein they reside."

"Ordered that Burrell Parkers mark be recorded (to wit.) a Swallow fork in the right Eare and a crop and half crop in the left Eare." Minutes of the Inferior Court of Pleas and Quarter Sessions, Johnston County, May 1775.

"In North Carolina they have Deer, Bears, Wild Cats, Opossums, Panthers, Alligators, Snakes in Abundance, & a very great Variety of other Animals. The female Opossum has a false Belly in which she breeds & protects her Young." "Journal of Ebenezer Hazard."

Jeremiah Norman was curious about the strange fauna in the new land he saw in his itinerant preaching. "We set out for Smith's Creek after early Breakfast . . . being very desirous to see the Amphibious Beast (called) allegator. A young man engaged to conduct me to a basking place of one. We were fully intending to kill him, if he were to be seen. The creek being narrow & crooked rendered our business intricate. We could not see him   only the place where he was when he flounced. I saw the rushes shake, & the water fly."

never entirely remove.

There were more of these human inhabitants than travelers often recognized at first. In 1770 an estimated 200,000 people lived in the province of North Carolina, and more newcomers were arriving every day. In the next twenty years, their numbers would nearly double, and North Carolina would rank third among the states in population. Deriving from a wide variety of ethnic and geographical backgrounds, North Carolina residents comprised a society of marked cultural diversity.

The oldest-settled section of the state was the region to the north of Albemarle Sound. Settlers from Virginia had spilled over into the region as early as the 1650s and had spread out steadily in the succeeding decades. Signs of Virginia influence persisted in the homes, speech, and customs they carried from the Sound region up the Roanoke, Tar, and Neuse river valleys. To the south, newcomers from South Carolina had penetrated the Cape Fear country in the first third of the eighteenth century. Members of the lowcountry gentry, these wealthy explorers established rice and indigo plantations like the ones they had left behind and also engaged in lumber and naval-stores production. The dominant whites of both the Albemarle and Cape Fear sections were heavily dependent on the labor of Negro slaves and brought numbers of Afro-Americans with them as they came.

The Cherokee Indians were the last major tribe to control a section of North Carolina. They were not forced to surrender the final remnant of their mountain homeland until 1835, but white settlement of the Piedmont, or backcountry as it was known, proceeded very rapidly in the 1750s and 1760s. Among the multitude of immigrants who found homes there, four groups were outstanding. Probably the largest number were Scotch-Irish, the descendants of Scottish Presbyterians who had colonized northern Ireland in the seventeenth century and moved from there to Pennsylvania and Maryland in the early eighteenth century. When population growth made these colonies seem crowded, second-generation families loaded their possessions into wagons and began to follow the Shenandoah Valley southwards in search of cheap and fertile land. They filled up western Virginia first and then began to flood the North Carolina Piedmont at mid-century.

A somewhat smaller group of German settlers followed the same pattern as the Scotch-Irish. Originally settled in the backcountry of Pennsylvania, where they became known as "Pennsylvania Dutch," the Germans sent new pioneers principally to the valleys of the Yadkin and Catawba rivers. Among them was the congregation of Moravians who founded the communities of Bethabara, Bethania, and Salem in the territory they called "Wachovia." A patchwork of German and Scotch-Irish settlements soon covered the Piedmont,

Early settlers arriving in North Carolina. Courtesy William S. Powell.

The Francis McNairy House, Greensboro Historical Museum, Guilford County, is a Scotch-Irish frame house now restored to its 1780s form, though it was originally built as a one-story structure during the 1760s.

The Dolley Madison Memorial is a restored German log house (ca. 1781), Greensboro Historical Museum, Guilford County. The central chimney accommodates an open hearth in the kitchen and an iron stove in the parlor. Its huge stack helped heat the upper story.

giving rise to alternating patterns of churches and place-names, such as Dutch Buffalo and Irish Buffalo creeks in present-day Cabarrus County.

Unlike other backcountry settlers, the Highland Scots came directly to North Carolina from the Old World. Changing British policies in Scotland had disrupted the middle and lower ranks of Highland society, and a fever for migration swept the region in the 1760s and 1770s. Disembarking at Wilmington, the Gaelic-speaking and kilt-clad strangers made for the upper reaches of the Cape Fear River, where they populated the new counties of Bladen, Cumberland, and Anson.

The fourth body of settlers were natives of eastern North Carolina, Virginia, or other northern colonies who were mostly of English origins. They spread throughout the Piedmont without ever calling attention to themselves as a separate ethnic entity. Most of these English descendants were respectable but otherwise anonymous pioneers. Some were Quakers from Pennsylvania and Nantucket. Certain others were wealthy and well-connected men who stepped very quickly into positions of civic, economic, and military leadership in the area.

Regardless of their origins, each divergent ethnic group had customs, manners, practices, and beliefs that distinguished it from

Even slaves in Moore County spoke Gaelic. When a visiting lowland Scot could not speak Gaelic, the slaves thought he was an imposter.

"A North Carolina Gaelic Bard," John McCrae, came from Scotland in 1774 and wrote a lullaby in his native Gaelic, part of which says:

"Sleep softly, my darling beloved,
Stay as you are, now that you're in a
    new land.
We'll find suitors abounding in wealth
    and fame,
And if you are worthy you shall have one
    of them.

In America now are we,
In the shade of the forest for ever
    unfailing.
When the winter departs and the warmth
    returns,
Nuts and apples and the sugar will
    grow."

the others. The Scots and the Germans spoke their own national languages, while Scotch-Irish, Quakers, and Moravians each cherished a special form of worship. The Africans and Indians were both sustained and stigmatized by their non-European cultural heritage. By the first quarter of the nineteenth century, however, there was a definite tendency for many of these unique characteristics to fade. Especially among the whites, the wilderness environment exerted a constant pressure on the residue of ethnic distinctiveness. An elderly grandparent or a handful of personal heirlooms was often all that kept alive the memory that identified this family as Scottish, that one as German, this other one as English by way of Virginia. Even among blacks, external conditions first broke down differences among diverse African tribesmen and then eased the distinction between "Guinea Negroes" and the "country-born" slaves who had only known life in America. A similar process seems to have happened among many Indians, as survivors of the decimated eastern tribes banded together in swamps, with no other common language but the white man's English. The ordinary business of survival brought about the creation of three distinct but overlapping southern cultures among whites, blacks, and Indians, each one centered on the land and the tasks that made it fruitful.

A harmonious relationship between human beings and nature was particularly important in the traditional culture of the American Indians. A combination of simple agriculture and hunting and gathering food from the forest environment enabled the Indians to maintain themselves comfortably without making heavy demands on the land or its resources. The arrival of massive numbers of whites made the Indians' way of life increasingly precarious because the intensive land-use patterns of the Europeans were incompatible with the Indians' farming and hunting practices. Even when the Indians showed a willingness to change their customs and to imitate the white men's economy, however, white hostility to the Indian presence ultimately drove the native Americans to the hidden, unwanted corners of the country—to the swamps of eastern North Carolina, to the peaks and valleys of the Great Smoky Mountains, or to the unsettled lands beyond the Mississippi River. In 1770, however, the grim alternatives of flight, expulsion, or extinction as a culture were still far-away threats to the Cherokees, North Carolina's largest and most powerful Indian tribe. Today, the Eastern Band of Cherokees demonstrate their eighteenth-century way of life at the Oconaluftee Indian Village, a living museum of their Qualla Boundary Reservation in Swain County, close by a major entrance to the Great Smoky Mountains National Park.

Centuries before the arrival of the whites, the Cherokees had migrated to the southern Appalachians from the northern regions of what is now the United States. Like the other eastern Indians, the

Cherokees lived in permanent towns of twenty to sixty families. They relied on large tracts of unoccupied forest for hunting grounds and for new fields when the older plots had lost fertility. In 1735 a white trader named James Adair put their numbers at 16,000, and counted sixty-four Cherokee towns in what is now western North Carolina, eastern Tennessee, upper South Carolina, and northern Georgia. By 1795 war and smallpox had taken a severe toll of Cherokee lives, and the tribe was reduced to forty-three towns and 2,500 warriors, or perhaps 6,700 persons altogether.

Like earlier Cherokee towns, the Oconaluftee Indian Village is located beside a stream and is surrounded by a high palisade of logs and earth. Traditional Cherokee townsmen had to protect themselves against a variety of enemies, both white and red. Within the walls, skilled men and women demonstrate the crafts that were essential for tribal survival. The visitor can see pots made from coils of clay and then baked to waterproof hardness before an open fire. Traditional dyeing, weaving, basket-making, beadwork, and food preparation are among the women's other tasks, while men demonstrate how arrow points were chipped from flint and canoes were hollowed out from poplar logs. Traditional traps for bear, quail, and fish are also on display, as are a variety of artifacts pertaining to Cherokee medicine, religion, and warfare.

Corn was the mainstay of the traditional Cherokee diet. Women planted the grain in hills and tilled it with simple hoes. They cooked corn into a popular mush and less frequently into bread. Women beat the kernels in large mortars with pestles made of logs. They shaped the resulting meal into loaves and baked them on hot stones, covered by large earthenware bowls. The women also planted beans, pumpkins, and squashes among the cornstalks, and added to their families' diets by gathering wild fruits, nuts, and other edible plant foods from the forest. Some of the village fields were tended in common by all the inhabitants while others were the special property of individual clans or kinship groups.

Meat for the village came from game killed primarily by men. Deer, bear, bison, and smaller game were the favorite quarry of Cherokee hunters. The men used bows and arrows and later guns to secure these animals in twice-yearly hunting expeditions. After making the proper sacrifices, they dried or barbecued the meat in the forest before bringing it home to the village. Fish were also important to the Cherokees. Villagers gathered them from mountain waters with spears carved from split canes, hooks fashioned from deer bones, and fish traps woven from reeds, splints, and canes.

The Cherokees' way of life made them keenly aware of the close connection between human life and the natural environment. Rituals and ceremonies helped to remind the tribe of the importance of the delicate relationship between man and the forests, the animals, and

Junaluska. N.C. State Archives. A band of Cherokees under Chief Junaluska helped Andrew Jackson win the Battle of Horseshoe Bend, 1814, ending the Creek War and opening what became the cotton states to white settlement. Though he suffered removal over the Trail of Tears in 1838, he returned to North Carolina to live among the Qualla remnant. A grateful state eventually recognized his services with a land grant and legal citizenship. Though over ninety, he witnessed the legislature's action and addressed his thanks to both its chambers. A lake resort in Haywood County preserves his name.

The Cherokees believed that disease was animals' retaliation for man's hunting them; each one contributed a specific ailment. But they also believed that plants took pity on man and each offered a cure to counteract a specific disease. Hence, the Indians depended heavily on herbal remedies.

"After I had dined, towards evening, a company of Indian girls, inhabitants of a village in the hills at a small distance, called, having baskets of strawberries; and this man, who kept here a trading house, being married to a cherokee woman of family, was indulged to keep a stock of cattle, and his helpmate being an excellent housewife, and a very agreeable woman, treated us with cream and strawberries." William Bartram's *Travels.*

the earth. While the Cherokees held very few formal religious beliefs as such, they were anxious to maintain themselves in a state of ritual purity and continued harmony with the various forces of nature. Conjurers and other magical experts specialized in the ceremonial practices that were intended to preserve these propitious conditions.

The most important festival of the year was the Green Corn Ceremony, held when the first ears of corn became edible. Fasting, purifying drinks, and repeated bathings were followed by sacrifices of the first fruits of corn and meat, and then by a round of feasting and dancing. When the corn became fully ripe, a second, longer round of dancing and thanksgiving began and continued for five days.

Hunting customs also taught the Cherokees to respect the fruitfulness of the earth and the fundamental unity of all living things. Fasting, bathing, and purification preceded and followed all major hunts. The conjurer sacrificed the tongue of the first deer killed to insure success in the remainder of the hunt. The Cherokees wore masks representing animals and covered themselves with the skins of their prey, not only to approach them undetected, but also to establish a magical affinity with the animal being sought. When bear were the quarry, special precautions were taken, for tribal legends taught that bear had once been men who had forgotten the importance of avenging the deaths of their own kinsmen. Bear had thus become fair game for people, but the Cherokee was careful first to ask the bear's permission before taking its life.

Cherokee culture was closely tied to the land and its resources, but the Cherokee way of life was not immune to change. Tribal customs altered significantly as Indian contact with whites increased. Three kinds of houses in Oconaluftee illustrate this evolutionary development. The earliest Cherokee homes were built of sapling logs stuck upright in the earth in the shape of a rectangle. The walls were formed like the sides of a basket, by canes woven around the logs and then plastered inside and out by clay mixed with grass. Slabs of bark laid over light rafters formed the roof. The door was a simple opening and there were no windows; a fire burned on the packed-earth floor but no chimney carried away the smoke. Later in the eighteenth century, Cherokees began to make cabins out of notched logs like the white settlers. These buildings had chimneys made of sticks covered with mud. When iron tools became widely available in Cherokee country, hewn square-sided logs and oak shingles went into a third style of Cherokee construction.

The families who lived in these houses puzzled European onlookers, who were used to an overwhelmingly male-dominated society. Cherokee men and women specialized in different tasks, but each participated in the particular activities of the other. Men thus concentrated on hunting and fighting, but they aided women with the heavier work in the fields. More surprising to Europeans, certain

A Cherokee demonstrating the ancestral technique of canoe-making at Oconaluftee Indian Village, Cherokee, Swain County.

Cherokee women took part in the hunt, spoke out in war councils, and decided the fate of prisoners of war. There were seven clans among the Cherokees; individuals in the same clan were considered too closely related to marry each other. Most Cherokee men took only one wife at a time, but divorce was distressingly frequent and casual from the point of view of missionaries and other reforming whites. Some reported that a Cherokee might take up with three different spouses in a year, but this was not the usual practice. Children belonged to their mother's clan, and individual houses and fields belonged to women, not men. In the event of a separation, the man returned to the maternal relatives of his own clan, while the woman continued to control her own property and offspring. Pre-

Reconstructed Indian cabin (after 1776), Oconaluftee Indian Village.

On seeing the ostentatious Tryon Palace, Jeremiah Norman was reminded of the Indian saying, "White men build great & fine Houses as if they were to live allways, but white men must die as well as Red men."

ferring the patriarchal customs of his own society, the English trader James Adair found a more equal relationship between the sexes disturbing and claimed that the Cherokees suffered from "petticoat government."

Contrary to Adair's supposition, men held the preponderant influence in Cherokee public affairs. The Council House at Oconaluftee is a replica of the building that stood in every Cherokee town and in which all major public decisions were made. It has seven sides and contains tiers of benches circling the council fire, which stands on an oval mound of earth in the center. During meetings and ceremonies, each of the seven clans sat in a body on its own side of the chamber. Presiding over the discussions and the rituals were two chiefs, one who governed in time of peace and another who commanded the town's warriors in battle. Real decisions were made by consensus, and the chiefs' main authority was based on the respect they commanded for their valor or their wisdom.

The most important decisions taken at the Council House were those pertaining to war. The Cherokees were inveterate fighters and no youth was considered fully grown until he had taken his first captive or claimed his first scalp. When the British asked the Cherokees to seek a truce with neighboring tribesmen, the chiefs refused, saying "we cannot live without war. Should we make peace with the Tuscaroras, with whom we are at war, we must immediately look for some other, with whom we can be engaged in our favorite occupation." Unlike the whites, however, the Cherokees did not make war to gain national advantages or to conquer a permanent empire. Their principal objective was retaliation and prestige. If a clan had lost a certain number of kinsmen in battle, it was the responsibility of the surviving clan members to avenge the deaths by inflicting an equal number of casualties in return. The occasional captive who escaped death by torture lived on as the slave of the warrior who had taken him.

A striking difference between white and Indian culture lay in their respective attitudes toward wealth and material possessions. Before the arrival of whites, Cherokees traded with other tribes for needed materials, but they did not expect to gather a larger and larger surplus every year in order to trade for a profit. The tribe gathered food and meat for their yearly needs but no more than that. Indeed, personal property was buried with the dead and household possessions were destroyed annually in a major ceremony marking the beginning of the year. Because there was no incentive to use the labor of others to accumulate surplus property, slaves did not work much harder than their masters. A slave thus increased his master's prestige but not his wealth. In fact, Cherokee men kept few possessions of any kind besides clothing, weapons, and the trophies of battle because fields belonged to women and scratching in the dirt in search of useless riches was beneath the dignity of a warrior. Initially,

William Bartram described the Council House as "a large rotunda, capable of accommodating several hundred people. It stands on the top of an ancient artificial mount of earth about twenty feet perpendicular, and the rotunda on the top of it, being above thirty feet more, gives the whole fabric an elevation of about sixty feet from the common surface of the ground."

Council House, Oconaluftee Indian Village.

Inside the Council House are masks and feathered robes, rich in religious symbolism closely tied to the Indians' natural environment.

the white man's love of acquisition invoked only the contempt of the Cherokees.

The Indians' resistance to commercial activity began to erode as soon as white soldiers and traders could demonstrate the superior qualities of European technology. Woolen cloth and iron tools had obvious advantages over buckskin and chipped-flint implements, while the power of muskets over bows and arrows could not be denied. In order to purchase the white man's products, Indians began to gather and sell the commodities desired by the whites. By 1735 James Adair estimated that the Cherokees were supplying him and the other traders with over a million pelts a year, the largest number of which were deerskins. Cherokees also learned to sell their human property.

The famous Cherokee Sequoyah, depicted with his syllabary, which he devised to enable his people to become literate. N.C. State Archives. The giant sequoias of Sequoia National Park are named for him.

Instead of destroying their prisoners of war in ceremonial tortures, Cherokees dabbled in the slave trade and supplied the South Carolina traders with captive enemy tribesmen for resale to the West Indies. Eventually, game became scarce and white colonists became wary of Indian slaves, for bondsmen with aggrieved relatives beyond the frontier were dangerous investments compared to Africans, who left kith and kin beyond the ocean. Sometimes forced by war and later compelled by debt, Cherokees began selling the last commodity left to them: their land. Between 1777 and 1819 Cherokees ceded a total of 8,927 square miles to the whites in North Carolina alone. When the tribe was finally reduced to a tiny fragment of its once-expansive domain, opponents of further cessions finally forced a halt, and the Cherokees sold no more land until they were forcibly ejected from the southern Appalachians between 1836 and 1838.

Before the grim story of expulsion was completed, however, the Cherokees made a remarkable recovery as a people. More than any other tribe in the United States, they continued the policy of selective borrowing from white culture. They took up the practice of stock-raising and cotton cultivation, began to embrace the Christian religion, and sent their children to mission schools. Tribal leaders intermarried with whites and began to purchase slaves instead of selling them. These Cherokees soon adopted a life-style that was virtually indistinguishable from the upcountry planter aristocracy. During the same period, the Cherokee Nation adopted a code of written laws, transformed itself into a self-governing republic, and began to publish a tribal newspaper in English and Cherokee, using an alphabet invented by a mixed-blood Cherokee named Sequoyah. Most of these cultural innovations took place in northern Georgia, where commercial agriculture and its accompanying changes were more accessible and more practical. North Carolina Cherokees were more deeply isolated in the remote coves of the Great Smokies, where they clung tenaciously to a traditional way of life. Unfortunately, the Cherokees' success in Georgia aroused their white neighbors' hostility and, as an ultimate result, the whole body of the Cherokee Nation was forced to relocate beyond the Mississippi between 1835 and 1838. A handful of North Carolina Cherokees evaded the federal soldiers who were sent to escort them to Oklahoma, and it is their descendants who have reconstructed Oconaluftee Indian Village. For generations after the removal of most of their fellow tribesmen, the Eastern Band of Cherokee Indians maintained a subsistence economy in the depths of the North Carolina mountains.

One white missionary who lived among the North Carolina Cherokees in the years before removal reported that "their cabins are not much inferior to those of the whites of the neighborhood." Housing was not the only area of resemblance between Cherokee culture and the life-style of the pioneer white family. The large ma-

16

jority of these settlers were called "yeomen." People of this class were small farmers and livestock producers who owned their own land and tilled it with their own labor. Like the Indians, white yeomen had limited contact with the market economy and depended for subsistence on the yield of the fields and the surrounding forests. A series of small houses in the Piedmont and central Coastal Plain reveals repeatedly the patterns of wilderness adjustment experienced by these men and women and their families. One of the simplest examples now stands on the Alamance Battleground State Historic Site, the home of John Allen (1749–1826) and Rachel Stout Allen (1760–1840). Built in 1782, the house stood for many years on the Allen family farm near Snow Camp, but it was moved to its present site and restored in 1967.

When he was about thirteen years old, John Allen came to North Carolina with his widowed mother, Phoebe, and her four other children. The Allens were Pennsylvania Quakers and they were looking for six hundred acres of land that Phoebe's husband had acquired but never settled before his death. Mrs. Allen joined some of her late husband's relatives in the Cane Creek Friends Meeting in Orange County, but she soon remarried and moved to Holly Spring, in nearby Randolph County. When he came of age, it fell to young John to take up his father's land on Cane Creek in Orange County. After returning to Pennsylvania to find a bride, John Allen married Rachel Stout in 1779 and brought her back to North Carolina. Thereafter, his small and temporary house gave way to a more substantial log cabin that came to house five generations of his descendants.

The Allen House is a simple box of hand-hewn timbers. A massive stone chimney dominates one wall and an enclosed stairway climbs beside it to a loft above. Cracks between the logs are sealed with mud and grass, but window glass was costly and the Allens did without. Two doors, at front and back of the cabin, are the only sources of light and ventilation in the main room, though a tiny window, shuttered but unglazed, opens from an upstairs gable. Wide eaves of the shingle roof extend over each entrance to form substantial porches at each end of the house. Planks enclose one half of one porch to form a small third room that could variously serve as a storage area, a visitor's room, a post office, and a store. Of John and Rachel's twelve known children, ten grew to adulthood in the little cabin, although the oldest were married and gone when the youngest were not yet born. The shape of the house and the character of its furnishings indicate the life-style of this fairly typical yeoman family.

Many of the Allens' important household activities undoubtedly took place outdoors or on their cabin's broad porches. Both doors typically stood open to admit air and light, so children, pets, and chores must have flowed over the steps and onto the packed bare earth of the yard. Tidy housekeepers, the Allens carefully prevented

Smyth described the backwoodsman: "Their whole dress is . . . very singular, and not very different from that of the Indians; being a hunting shirt . . . ornamented with a great many fringes, tied round the middle with a broad belt, much decorated also, in which is fastened a tomahawk, an instrument that serves every purpose of defense and convenience; being a hammer at one side and a sharp hatchet at the other; the shot bag and powder-horn, carved with a variety of whimsical figures and devices, hang from their necks over one shoulder; and on their heads a flapped hat, of a reddish hue, proceeding from the intensely hot beams of the sun."

Allen House (ca. 1782), Alamance Battleground State Historic Site, Alamance County.

Cabin construction on the frontier showed ethnic variations. The English built one-room structures of sawn timber, sixteen-feet square, while the Scotch-Irish more usually built sixteen-by twenty-two-foot log cabins using German techniques.

the growth of grass or weeds near the house. Grass was a fire hazard and harbored insects; there was no simple way to trim it; and, perhaps most important, it was a symbol of nature that the pioneers were determined to keep at bay. At night or in bad weather, cooking, eating, sleeping, making clothes, mending tools, and learning lessons must have been concentrated in the cabin's one main room. Its furniture, much of which originally belonged to the Allens, reflects this combination of functions. Iron cooking utensils fill the hearth, while shelves and cupboards hold the dishes. Most of these were earthenware of local manufacture, but eighteen pewter spoons and eleven pewter vessels were among the family possessions as well. Other belongings were stored in chests, which must have served for seats as well because there were never enough chairs to go around. A loom fills one corner, while cards for preparing fibers and spinning wheels for twisting them into thread stand nearby. Opposite sits a bed for father and mother, with a trundle bed beneath for small children and a cradle at hand for the baby. Corn husk mattresses for the older children would have lain on the floor of the loft. Numerous travelers' accounts confirm that pioneer families routinely lived and even put up overnight guests in even more crowded conditions than these. In such close quarters, modern notions of privacy and separate personal space clearly had no chance to develop.

Like the all-purpose nature of their living space, the workaday life of the Allens was varied and had to accommodate a wide assortment of tasks and skills. No single career limited the scope of man's or woman's labor. John Allen was a teacher, for example, and regularly contracted with his neighbors to instruct their children in reading, writing, spelling, and arithmetic. Allen was also a farmer and a merchant, and, because he was blessed with good lands and the labor of eight sons, he had achieved a modest competence by the time of his death at the age of seventy-seven.

The papers relating to John Allen's estate show the range of his diverse work activities. The store held a very limited inventory, but

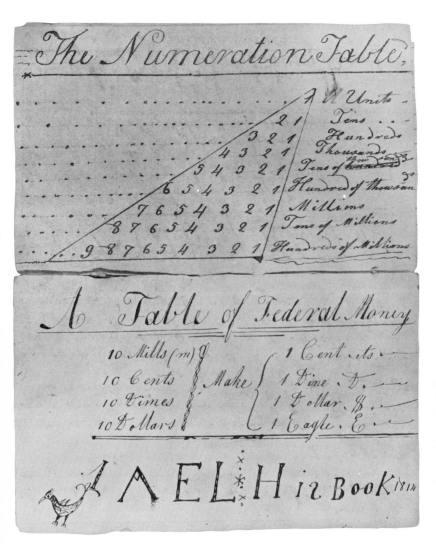

(Left) Tables from Alexander E. Lowrance's school notebook (1814). Thomas Lenoir Papers.

John Allen's pupils at Rock Spring School were prohibited from "baring the Master out of School," "pinching or picking at one a nother or lafing," or "Scribling on one a nothers Books," among a long list of rules of deportment. Allen, *Allen House and Some of its Allens.*

19

Candle-making was a regular chore of the endlessly busy housewife.

Rachel Allen's prescription for a "raging fit of [kidney] stone: Beat Onions into a pulp & apply them as a poultis part to the Back and part to Each Groin   it gives Speedy Ease in the most Racking pain." Allen, *Allen House and Some of its Allens*.

For cleaning the teeth, Rachel Allen advised rubbing them with ashes of burnt bread.

Allen House smokehouse.

shoppers could find yellow silk, satin, calico, buttons, pins, pencils, shoes, and hardware. The farm was more elaborate. Wheat, oats, and corn were the field crops, but five cattle, fifteen sheep, ten hogs, and two beehives were equally important for the family's well-being. A collection of shovels, hoes, pitchforks, scythes, and sickles were the tools for cultivating and harvesting these crops, and several hogs-heads were the receptacles for storing them. Allen owned a wagon to carry his grain to the mill and to haul any surplus to market, but there were no draft animals to pull it or to draw his three plows and one harrow. By the end of his life, the aging farmer was probably bor-rowing horses or oxen from his grown sons, each of whom was now established on a farm of his own, carved from the father's original land grant. A well-stocked chest of carpenter's tools rounded out the family's working gear. These were essential to shape the wood that formed so many items of daily use, but Allen may have done some work for hire as well.

The skills and labor of Rachel Allen were as varied and as essen-tial to family welfare as those of her husband. She bore twelve chil-dren and did the cooking, spinning, sewing, and mending for her burgeoning family. The yard of the Allen House contains a vegetable and herb garden and an ash hopper for making soap, both of which were Rachel's responsibility as well. These were the tasks of every pioneer housewife.

In addition, Rachel Allen grew very skilled in the uses of roots, herbs, and the traditional folk medicine of her neighborhood. Her services were much in demand in cases of illness, injury, and probably of childbirth as well, and she owned a riding mare to carry her to the homes of her many patients. Her notebook contains home remedies for burns, infected sores, warts, consumption, rheumatism, "bad blood," "yaws or Country distemper," kidney stones, palsy, "any Inward Weakness," even cancer. Rachel Allen's role as a healer was closely tied to her traditionally female duties as mother and nurse, but no professional restrictions or taboos prevented her from exer-cising her gifts to the fullest extent possible in her time and place. As a woman of skill and strength in the growing backcountry, her eco-nomic importance to the family was as essential and obvious as it was varied.

The combined efforts of John and Rachel Allen produced a com-fortable but very simple standard of living at the end of a long life together. Yeoman farmers back in England often had no choice but to bequeath all their real estate to the oldest son, in order to leave even one child with a farm large enough to support the next generation. The same conditions were coming to exist in some northern states, which may have been a reason why John's father had wanted to leave Pennsylvania. The North Carolina forest was kinder to the pioneer than those older environments. Dividing his lands into scrupulously equivalent legacies, John Allen left each son with an adequate farm and each child with an equal portion of cash. He had also loaned each son considerable amounts of money to get started and had probably been the source of tools and livestock as well. Daughters got less, not because they ranked lower in their father's esteem, but because Allen took for granted that all his children would marry and his daughters would benefit from their husbands' inheritances. The North Carolina experience gave John Allen an opportunity to do what might have been denied him elsewhere: a chance to treat his children with what he regarded as equality.

As a result of his bequests of land, John Allen's sons lived and raised their own families in a cluster of bordering farms in Orange and Chatham counties. They took an active role in Cane Creek and Holly Spring Friends Meetings, married women who were members of the same congregations (some of whom were their distant cousins) and generally shared their lives with the circle of friends and relatives who composed their respective communities. Rachel Allen presumably kept practicing her healing arts. She followed a circuit through her children's families, boarding with each son in successive intervals until she died in 1840. The Allen grandchildren grew up surrounded by aunts, uncles, and cousins, and with a grandmother who joined their households frequently. As these children looked out at the world, they saw an ever-widening set of concentric circles made up of immediate family members, close relatives, distant relatives, church members, and neighbors, with no strict distinctions between each group. The intermingling of family and community was surely a central part of how they learned to view the world and other people.

Just as John Allen's grandchildren saw society from a special viewpoint as they peered beyond his cabin, outsiders looking in also saw things from a particular perspective. Eighteenth-century travelers frequently found much to criticize in the life-styles they observed among the North Carolina yeomen. Such observers might have felt that the Allens' mud-chinked cabin was excessively drafty and dark. They might also have found fault with the spelling of John Allen, the self-certified schoolmaster, or questioned the efficacy of Rachel Allen's homemade potions. Those who came to Cane Creek from parts of the world where different conceptions of family were beginning to take hold might have thought to themselves that the Allens lacked a proper sense of privacy, and that personal living space was altogether too public for their own good and for the comfort of others. It is quite true that the Allens' standards of writing, medical treatment, and building differed from ours. But, though their house was small and seemingly crude, the Allens' acquisitions represented a solid achievement. John's persistent interest in education testified that his life on the frontier had not lapsed into unlettered barbarism. At the end of his life, three items had special meaning for John Allen

Ash hopper at the Allen House. Sara Haworth remembers how soap was made: "Our ancestors saved the wood ashes, put them in the lye hopper, poured water on them and the water dropped down into the ashes into this lye barrel. When it got strong enough to float an egg, it was strong enough to combine with the animal fat that had been saved and to make soap—and I am telling you, it was some soap! It would take the skin off of your hands." Haworth, *Museum of Old Domestic Life*.

21

Main room in the Allen House.

Perhaps Smyth exaggerated when he made the following observation, but perhaps he was noting a national characteristic in its earliest phase: "Even the most indigent person has his saddlehorse, which he rides to every place, and on every occasion; for in this country nobody walks on foot the smallest distance, except when hunting; indeed a man will frequently go five miles to catch a horse, to ride only one mile upon afterwards."

as symbols of his material and cultural accomplishments. A grandfather clock, a walnut Chippendale desk, and a collection of twenty books received special mention in his will. These handsome and expensive articles were to be auctioned off within the family, the proceeds to be divided with the other cash of the estate. The same clock and desk are in the house today. The juxtaposition of these luxuries with the simpler tools and furniture serve as an appropriate expression of the aspirations of one pioneer family as well as the limitations of the backcountry environment.

Because the Allens lived in the Piedmont, the desk and clock they treasured probably had come to them over a long rough wagon road from a distant market center like Fayetteville or Petersburg,

Virginia. The crops they grew in exchange for such comforts were likewise very tedious and expensive to haul away for sale. The cost of traveling back and forth to market ensured that families like the Allens would try their best to "live at home" by raising or making themselves the food, clothing, and other materials they used in daily life. They worked to raise a small surplus for sale only to get the necessary cash for taxes and for items like salt, sugar, or a clock that they could not make themselves. The Allens' tiny store kept them more closely tied to the market economy than most of their neighbors, but on the whole theirs was not a highly commercialized lifestyle. The Allens proved that this could be a reasonably comfortable way to live, but it was not the way to bring rapid economic growth to a family, a region, or a state. Growth required specialization on a cash crop or crops and a commitment to the market economy, but neither of these was practical while the Piedmont remained isolated. As long as transportation costs stayed high, John Allen's children and grandchildren would continue to live just as he had, and thoughtful observers would begin to note that Piedmont North Carolina was taking a remarkably long time to progress beyond the frontier stage of development.

Though hardly perfect, transportation in eastern North Carolina

Colonial money. N.C. State Archives.

On a visit to a Cape Fear plantation, the Scotswoman Janet Schaw was amused by the contrast between the poor house and its fine furnishings: "I assure you they keep a good house, tho' it is little better than one of his Negro huts, and it appeared droll enough to eat out of China and be served in plate in such a parlour. He has however an excellent library with fine globes and Mathematical instruments of all kinds, also a set of noble telescopes, and tho' the house is no house, yet the master and the furniture make you ample amends."

The Pender Museum (1810), the relocated and restored Everitt house, St. Andrew Street, Tarboro, Edgecombe County.

bettered that of the Piedmont. Numerous rivers and broad streams made navigable channels across the Coastal Plain. Once their rafts and flatboats arrived at market towns like Edenton, New Bern, and Wilmington, easterners still faced the hazards of getting past the Outer Banks, but at least the inland portions of their journeys were less difficult than for settlers farther west. Higher soil fertility and a longer length of settlement were further advantages for eastern North Carolina. During the late eighteenth century, eastern farmers took advantage of their opportunities to enjoy a somewhat higher standard of living than was common farther to the west, but these differences should not be exaggerated. As late as 1810 a Duplin County resident noted that, although a few "framed Clapboard Houses with Clay Chimneys" had replaced the inhabitants' original log cabins, "the greatest Number of the Citizens yet build in the old Stile." Even when a farmer found the money to build with sawn lumber instead of logs, the results were hardly grandiose. The Duplin writer emphasized that in spite of recent improvements "there are no Stone or Brick walled Homes, nor any that can be called Edifices in the County." Beneath some superficial details of materials and design, the similarities between yeoman farmers in the east and the west were at least as significant as the differences.

The building that is now called the Pender Museum in Tarboro illustrates the advantages eastern farmers enjoyed as well as the continued limitations that affected them. Silas and Rebecca Everitt built the small frame cottage about 1810, on their farm in the Conetoe community of eastern Edgecombe County. Farmers in that section were well known for their excellent pork, which thrived on the rich vegetation of surrounding swamps. The drier patches of light, sandy soil made fertile fields for corn, peas, potatoes, cotton, and flax. Careless of their soil's fine quality, landowners cleared new ground for fields, rapidly exhausted their fertility, abandoned them, and then cleared more. These wasteful methods were identical to those prevailing in the frontier sections of the west. Naval stores were also still important in Edgecombe County, and they and other products were floated down the Tar River in long flatboats for sale in the town of Washington.

Later in the antebellum period, Edgecombe's natural advantages would make it the leading cotton county in the state and a well-known center for the most advanced agricultural techniques. In Silas Everitt's time, the days of plantation glory were several decades away. In 1811, when the Everitts' house was still new, an Edgecombe County doctor could still say with a fair degree of accuracy that "the inhabitants of the county generally live comfortably; & in proportion to their industry, enjoy the luxuries of life. There are no overgrown 'estates' here; & there are comparatively few oppressed with poverty."

The farmhouse of Silas and Rebecca Everitt reflects this inter-

Bedroom of the Everitt house.

mediate stage of economic development. Heated by two brick chimneys and resting above the ground on brick foundations, the house was carefully designed for warmth in winter and ventilation in summer. The front door is flanked by two sash windows made of fifteen panes of glass, and every outside board has a handmade beaded edge for shedding rainwater. Finely turned columns support a shed porch projecting over the front door, and finely detailed molding highlights the eaves and cornices of the roof. These aesthetic and practical refinements were significant advances over the rough simplicity of the Allen House of Orange County.

A close inspection shows, however, that the Allens and the Everitts shared many ideas about how a house should look. The

Shed-room of the Everitt house.

Everitt House is a typical coastal cottage with a hall-and-parlor floor plan. Common throughout eastern North Carolina, this type of house is rectangular, with a long off-center partition dividing it into one large room—the "hall"—and one small room—the "parlor." A lean-to room projects from the rear, adding a third chamber to the downstairs. This old-fashioned design had come from England with the earliest Virginia colonists. The hall was used for most family activities, and the parlor was used for secondary purposes like storage.

Family living was much the same in both of these houses. The hall-and-parlor floor plan allowed these households only a slight degree of privacy. In the average-sized family, there were no separate rooms for sleeping and at least one bed probably sat in every room. Family members began to encounter household activity as soon as they approached the porch and plunged into the hubbub of personal life as soon as they crossed the threshold. Visitors faced the same conditions, for no neutral passageways guided a person from one part of the house to another, or screened the casual visitor from intimate family business.

Why did the Everitts and the Allens fail to hide from themselves and from their guests cooking food, drying laundry, crying children, and bedridden invalids? Was it simply because they could not afford to build "proper" houses? If so, why did Silas Everitt squander his means on beaded weatherboarding and similar luxuries? Were these families simply primitive backwoodsmen who did not know any better? John Allen's desk, clock, and books testify to the contrary. It is more likely that the Allens and the Everitts both built their houses in ways that reflected contemporary attitudes toward family living. Like most other eighteenth-century men and women, they made few sharp distinctions between what was public and what was private, between what was suitable to show the outside world and what ought to be kept invisible, even from the family itself.

Not only were there striking similarities in the life-styles of eighteenth-century yeoman farmers in eastern and western North Carolina, but there was also a common—and a distinctly premodern —concept of family existence. The Allens and the Everitts did not live in specialized spaces, nor did they lead compartmentalized lives. Each family had the skills to perform a variety of tasks and when possible they performed these tasks themselves. There was no rigid line between the world of the workplace and the world of the family because almost all work was done at home by parents and children. Nor was each household an isolated unit. Each farm stood by itself at some distance from its neighbors, but the individual households of parents and children were relatively open to temporary members like grandmother Rachel Allen. Moreover, the extended family blended imperceptibly outward into a surrounding community of relatives. Property lines were kept distinct, but other boundary lines were

The Boggan-Hammond House, Wadesboro, Anson County.

blurred in this society, just as they were in the physical space within
the cabins. All was not sweetness and light in such communities;
there could be overwhelming pressures on individuals to live and to
think by a community consensus, or fierce and deadly feuds could
erupt out of so much togetherness. But, if the Allens were a representative family, the general effect of this way of life was first to
recreate and then to preserve a traditional sense of family and rural
community coherence that harked back to the peasant societies of
Europe. Unlike their European and New England counterparts, these
southern white yeomen did not live in physically compact villages,
but a distinctive sense of community was equally central to their
world view.

Other small homes of the late eighteenth century show variations of the characteristics apparent in the Allen and Everitt houses.
The Boggan-Hammond House (1783) and the John Haley House
(1786) are town and country examples of other Piedmont construction. These houses supplied basically the same amount of living
space. Though humbly born but successful men could join the elite in
the backcountry, particularly after the Revolution, serious economic
obstacles prevented their achieving more than a modest standard
of living. One feature of the Haley House design corresponds to that
of the Allen House: each house had one room other than the main
room that could be entered from the outside. This made them independent of the activities in the main room of each house and presaged
the attempt to separate family and work that would become more
common in the century that followed.

The Hezekiah Alexander House (1774),
Mint Museum of History, Charlotte,
Mecklenburg County, reflects the Pennsylvania and Maryland building tradition
its owner knew in his youth.

28

Planters and Slaves

Hezekiah Alexander was yet another immigrant from the north who moved to Piedmont North Carolina in the 1760s. Alexander was a Presbyterian and he came from Scotch-Irish stock, but the other contours of his life were remarkably similar to those of yeomen like John Allen and John Haley. He was born in 1728 in Cecil County, Maryland, not far from the Pennsylvania border. Like Allen, his grandfather had come from Ireland to the Delaware River Valley in the seventeenth century. His father became a man of some substance in his neighborhood, but Hezekiah and six other of his father's fifteen children eventually tried their luck in Mecklenburg County, North Carolina. Hezekiah Alexander was a blacksmith who bought land and became a farmer and cattle grower. He died in 1801, survived by his wife and nine of their ten children, having earned an enviable position as an elder in his church and a distinguished Revolutionary patriot.

Dining room of the Alexander House, which features substantial furniture and handsome paneling.

The most obvious difference between Hezekiah Alexander and his yeoman counterparts was his house. Known as the "Rock House," it stands on its original site in the present city limits of Charlotte and forms a part of the Mint Museum of History. The Rock House is two-and-a-half stories high with a dressed stone exterior and two interior stone chimneys. There are three rooms downstairs; each one is heated by its own fireplace. The upstairs and downstairs are well lighted by many large glazed windows; there are even several small windows in the attic. Alexander's estate inventory showed comparable signs of affluence: a silver watch and a series of loans to sons and other borrowers. Unlike his contemporaries, John Allen and Silas Everitt, Hezekiah Alexander cut quite a figure in the world.

The probable explanation for Alexander's good fortune appears in the clauses of his will. "I give unto my said wife Mary two negro men viz: Sam & Abram and four Work Horses her choice. . . . I likewise give and bequeath unto my wife Mary her Bed & furniture her mare and Saddle and all the Dresser furniture and one Negro Woman Bet to her and her assigns forever." Similar bequests of human property were made to five of Alexander's nine surviving children; the others had apparently received slaves when they married.

For most ambitious men, labor was the key to riches in eighteenth-century North Carolina. There was plenty of land available at cheap prices; the secret was to find workers who could make it pay. A father lost his children's labor as soon as they reached adulthood, and few white men would work very long for wages when land could be had practically for the asking. For the man who was determined to

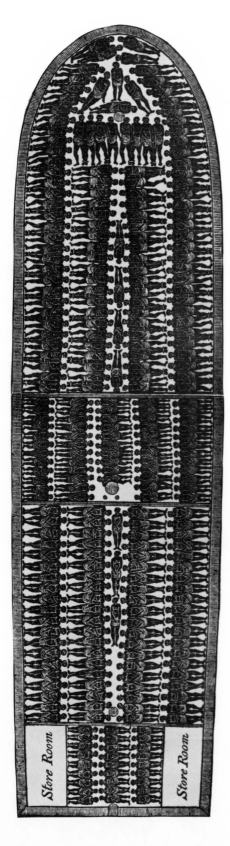

Store Room

Store Room

accumulate more property than he could earn by his own efforts, slaves were the solution. Silas Everitt owned none in 1810 but by 1820 he had acquired a slave family of four: a man, a woman, and two small boys. John Allen owned no slaves. Hezekiah Alexander owned as many as thirteen slaves, a number which placed him in the top 1 percent of householders in late eighteenth-century Mecklenburg County. Alexander's labor force was the simple fact that accounted for the difference of scale between his Rock House and the more modest dwellings of nonslaveholders.

Slavery had been a part of North Carolina society from its beginning. The leading Lords Proprietors had been planters and slave traders in the West Indies and they included the "peculiar institution" in their plans for their mainland colony. In Virginia and South Carolina, slave plantations were central features of society from the early eighteenth century onwards. Cultivating tobacco in the north and rice in the south, slave labor in North Carolina's bordering colonies paid for the beautiful homes and elegant life-styles of the colonial aristocracy. The same geographical handicaps that kept many yeomen out of the planter class kept North Carolina's smaller number of slaveholders from reaching the levels of affluence enjoyed by their counterparts to the north and south. As a result, the plantation system in North Carolina was never so fully developed as it was elsewhere. Nevertheless, slavery was crucial to the character of North Carolina society.

Nonslaveholding white farmers and herdsmen were the most numerous group in the population, but slaveholders were the wealthiest and most powerful citizens, while the slaves themselves were central participants in the emergence of a common southern culture. In some eastern counties, blacks were a majority of the local population by the mid-eighteenth century. Even the Cherokee Indians adopted the practice of slaveholding. The presence of these slaves had a powerful impact, moreover, on the feelings of the nonslaveholding whites. Yeoman farmers might aspire to become slaveholders themselves, they might come to resent blacks as symbols of the planter's superior advantages, or they could fear blacks as potential competitors or enemies of all white people. Most likely their attitudes could embrace all of these emotions to one degree or another. Though relatively limited in its extent, slavery touched the lives of all North Carolinians.

Most North Carolina Negroes came originally to the province from other British colonies. As Governor George Burrington had reported in 1733, "as none come directly from Affrica, we are under a necessity to buy, the refuse, refractory and distemper'd Negroes, brought from other Governments." Burrington's assumption that most blacks involved in the intercolonial slave trade were sold for some defect of their own was questionable, but it does appear that most imported slaves came singly or in small groups to North Carolina. One correspondent of the Blount brothers, for example, paid off his debts with human property. "I have shiped on board the sloop Washington Capt. Kirbey a Negro Boy named David who is a Smart Active fellow," wrote James Aiken of Philadelphia. "Part of his time Imployed as a waiter which he is very expert in," Aiken explained, "& Lukwise [likewise] Understands farming well. . . . please pay the Amt. of what you may sell him for after Expenses Deducted to [Mr. Barr]." Torn away from his family and friends by the caprice of a commercial economy, David brought his diverse talents as a house servant and fieldhand to a still-unpolished society with a great demand for all types of skill.

Not all the slaves who came to North Carolina experienced previous periods of adjustment in another colony. On 10 June 1786 the brig *Camden* docked at Edenton, her hold packed with eighty African men and women, brought directly from the Guinea coast. "They talk a most curious lingo," one observer remarked, and "are extremely black, with elegant white teeth." The newcomers were all between twenty and twenty-five years old, they had each cost £ 28 sterling, and the observer added, they were clad only "in a state of nature." These naked and frightened young people were the property of Josiah Collins, an English-born merchant of Edenton who had recently formed a partnership with two other gentlemen to dig a canal from Lake Phelps, in Washington County, to the Scuppernong River. Known as the Lake Company, the partners intended to sell lumber from the surrounding swampland and to raise rice on the thick alluvial muck that the timbering and draining operations would uncover. The canal would be essential to carry both types of products to a market. Joined by other slaves from the neighborhood, the newly arrived Africans were to be the essential work force for the Lake Company's ambitious undertaking.

Collins and his partners built their canal. Still visible today, it stretches for six miles, twenty feet wide and six feet deep, through the otherwise impenetrable fastness of the Great Alligator Dismal Swamp. Water flowing through the canal turned sawmills and gristmills and powered sophisticated corn-shelling and wheat-threshing equipment. A network of ditches and sluices drained the surrounding fields of corn, wheat, and rice, and, when necessary, flooded the latter with water from the lake. The canal and its machinery became the economic focal point for a cluster of plantations on the shores of Lake Phelps, the largest of which was Josiah Collins's Somerset Place.

Now a state historic site, Somerset Place was the property in turn of the original Josiah Collins, his son Josiah Collins, Jr., and his grandson Josiah Collins III. The mansion that stands there today was built for Josiah Collins III around 1830. For the Collins slaves, Somerset Place was home from the late 1780s until the era of the Civil War.

(Left). Drawing of the slave ship *Brookes. An Abstract of the Evidence Delivered before a Select Committee of the House of Commons in the Years 1790 and 1791* (London, 1791).

Robert Hunter, Jr., noted in 1785 that Collins "expects to finish it [the canal] by Christmas if it ceases raining . . . in keeping 150 slaves daily at work. The expense, he says, will be 3,000 at least, but when the work is accomplished he will have cleared 100,000 acres of the finest woodland that almost was ever known (oak, sycamore, popular, cypress, etc.)—which is an amazing object and a very great undertaking."

Later representation of a slave cabin.
N.C. State Archives.

Surviving business records and an ongoing program of archeological investigation make it possible to reconstruct the pattern of their work and daily life with some assurance.

The "Guinea Negroes" who arrived in Edenton in 1786 had probably been captured in a tribal war as many as several hundred miles inland from the west African coast. They had survived a grueling march to the ocean and a harrowing three- or four-month voyage across the Atlantic known as the Middle Passage. Many others had no doubt died from these experiences; many more died from the ordeal of digging the canal.

The work was exhausting and dangerous. Joined by an almost equal number of "country-born" slaves who had grown up in the New World, the Africans were forced to clear timber, to remove the earth from the bed of the canal, and to construct a road to run beside it. When Charles William Jansen, an English businessman, visited a similar canal project in adjoining Hyde County, he found a "gang of about sixty negroes, whose daily work was in water, often up to the middle, and constantly knee-deep." This waterway was the venture of the tireless Blount brothers, entrepreneurs in so many different efforts, but conditions at Lake Phelps could not have been much different. Work progressed so slowly there that the task that the Lake Company had hoped to finish by Christmas of 1786 stretched on until 1789.

According to their overseer, disease, overwork, and exposure took a heavy toll of African lives. By his account, "when they were disabled they would be left by the bank of the canal, and the next morning the returning gang would find them dead." Those who withstood the physical demands of their work sometimes succumbed to the psychological strain of homesickness and wrenching personal disruption. "At night they would begin to sing their native songs," the overseer reported, "and in a short while would become so wrought up that, utterly oblivious to the danger involved, they would grasp their bundles of personal effects, swing them on their shoulder, and setting their faces towards Africa, would march down into the water singing as they marched till recalled to their senses only by the drowning of some of the party." Unwilling to lose his laborers, Collins soon forbade these demonstrations.

Not all of Collins's slaves came directly from Africa. He had imported eighty adults in 1786 but the company apparently intended to put at least a hundred and fifty laborers to work on the canal project. The remaining slaves seem to have been brought in from the partners' other farms in the Albemarle area or purchased from smaller farmers nearby. Already acclimated to American diseases, the "country-born" slaves probably lived through the first years in greater numbers than the Africans. Few of the Africans seem to have lived until 1839, when the first surviving slave inventory for Somerset

Place was prepared.

One who did live that long was Guinea Jack, who crossed the ocean when he was about eighteen years old. We can reconstruct the main outlines of this Carolinian's life from the information recorded about him in the 1839 inventory. Not many years after he arrived at the lake, Guinea Jack married Fanny, who was about the same age or a little older. She gave birth to a son named Will in 1790. As he would have in his African homeland, Guinea Jack took a second wife, Grace, who became the mother of Sam in 1797. The two wives presented their husband with a least one child each in the years ahead. African polygamy was not typical in the slave community, but it was not altogether unheard-of or unconventional either. Guinea Jack's children learned both an African and an Afro-American cultural tradition from their parents and represented the fusion of the slave communities that gradually developed at Somerset Place.

Other signs of cultural blending appeared in the areas of language and religion. After the Civil War, a local physician, Dr. Edward Warren, recalled that the elderly Africans at Somerset Place used to speak "a medley of their original dialect and the English language, and to me [it] was perfectly unintelligible." The Africans of 1786 may have belonged to the same ethnic group and spoken the same language, but the Afro-Americans of the Albemarle region spoke English. As a result, the slaves probably combined elements of both tongues in a pidgin language to use with each other. Dr. Warren also reported that the Somerset slaves adopted Christianity in the nineteenth century, but that the African-born slaves, as he put it, "still had faith in evil genii, charms, spirits, philters, metempsychosis, etc., and they habitually indulged in an infinitude of cabalistic rites and ceremonies in which the gizzards of chickens, the livers of dogs, the heads of snakes and the tails of lizards played a mysterious but very conspicuous part." The doctor's tone was patronizing, but it is clear from his account that traditional African religious practices flourished alongside Christianity for many decades.

A striking example of African culture survived in the "John Kooner" ceremony, which the slaves at Somerset performed every Christmas morning. A leading man of the slave community would disguise himself in a garb of rags and animal skins. Joined by another slave in American Sunday-style clothing, "John Kooner" would lead a large group of followers to the master's house. Accompanied by drumming, dancing, and chanting, the pair demanded money from the master, mistress, and all white residents of the plantation. Success was followed by a general celebration in the slave quarters. The John Kooner ritual appeared on other eastern North Carolina plantations and also among slaves in Jamaica. The drums, the dancing, the chants, and the costume seem clearly derived from Africa. When they used an African ceremony to extract money from their masters,

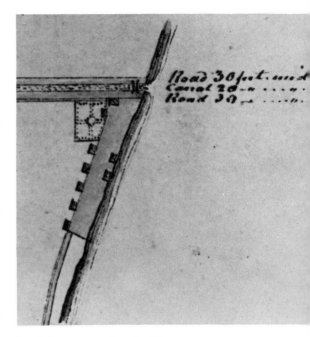

Detail from survey (1821) of Somerset Plantation showing the original orientation of the slave cabins along the lakefront. N.C. State Archives.

33

the Somerset slaves reversed the normal social order of the plantation and reaffirmed their own dignity as independent human beings. Cultural expressions of black humanity were a vital part of the slaves' resistance to the psychological burdens of life in bondage.

From the earlier days of the Lake Company, the Somerset slave community lived in a row of cabins that extended away from the canal along the lakeshore. The remains of these buildings have not yet been found, so we cannot be sure of living conditions at Somerset Place in the eighteenth century. When they did make note of it, most contemporary observers seemed to think that slaves lived in buildings that were similar to those of poor settlers generally. An anonymous Scottish author thought slaves were quite comfortable. "They have small houses or huts, like peasants, thatched, to which they have little gardens, and live in families, separated from each other," "Scotus Americanus" assured the readers of his "Informations concerning the Province of North Carolina." Writing in 1811, Dr. Jeremiah Battle of Edgecombe County was less sanguine and believed that slave housing was conducive to poor health. According to Dr. Battle, "The negro huts [in Scotland Neck] are generally built of round pine or cypress logs, with dirt floors, & dirt in the interstices between the logs. They are small, crowded, & smoky; & as might be expected very filthy." Leading medical authorities were aware of the connection between cleanliness and disease, but many eighteenth-century slaveowners were not. Farsighted masters might insist that quarters be kept sanitary and be certain that slaves had ample time for housecleaning, but others viewed the hours spent away from field labor as a waste of valuable time.

Slave food was like slave housing—adequate to sustain life but far from satisfying. According to Charles William Jansen, the weekly allowance of Thomas Blount's slaves in Hyde County "consisted of *salt herrings*, of an inferior quality, and a peck of *Indian corn in the cob*, to each." When Jansen visited their quarters, the Blount slaves had not received salt beef or pork for months, "and Mr. Overseer, with perfect indifference, observed, that he did not expect any fresh supply for some time after what was brought them should be consumed." William Attmore and other eighteenth-century travelers agreed that the typical slave ration in eastern North Carolina included a peck of corn per week, and sometimes an additional portion of salted fish or meat. The food furnished by masters provided slaves with an adequate number of calories for each worker but neither variety nor an adequate supply of vitamins. Nutritional requirements were not well understood in the eighteenth century, and dietary deficiency diseases were consequently common among lower-income white and black North Carolinians until well into the twentieth century.

Archeological investigation at Somerset Place has provided evidence that slave diet there was not strictly limited to the rations issued by Josiah Collins. Foundations of a large kitchen and storehouse complex have been uncovered that seem to have been used as a food preparation area from the earliest days of the plantation. Bones of butchered cows, pigs, deer, turtles, and other animals appeared in the remains, indicating that slaves were able to supplement their diet with their own hunting and stock-raising efforts. Black bean fragments testify to additional vegetable items on the slave table. The slaves who dug the canal were probably fed communally from this kitchen or one like it.

Travelers' accounts confirm that many masters provided a minimum ration to slave families and expected their bondsmen to supplement these supplies from their own gardens. "Scotus Americanus" reported that slaves on the lower Cape Fear were given a daily task that could be finished by the early afternoon. Afterward, they were free to cultivate plots provided by the master, to hunt, to fish, or otherwise occupy their time independently. Each family received "5 or 6 acres each, for rice, corn, potatoes, tobacco &c. for their own use and profit, of which the industrious among them make a great deal." Janet Schaw agreed with his observation and added calabashes and other vegetables to the list of slave produce. Later generations of Collins slaves raised corn in a "Negro patch" behind their quarters, though their work for the master normally kept them in his fields until sundown.

Some slaves raised hogs and poultry that they sold to the master at current prices, and spent their earnings on clothing, pocketknives, and other personal items. "Scotus Americanus" was sure that the slaves worked on their own plots "for amusement, pleasure, and profit," and not for subsistence, but, in view of what others have said about slave rations, his interpretation seems overly generous. Making slaves responsible for feeding themselves was too good a disciplinary device for most masters to pass up. It was also in the master's interest to be sure that his slaves were not kept hungry, for if they did not feel well-fed, most slaves did not hesitate to steal what they needed from a tightfisted owner.

Eighteenth-century slaves were less successful in clothing themselves than they were in finding enough to eat. While traveling through Craven, Carteret, and Onslow counties on 8 January 1778, Ebenezer Hazard wrote in his diary that he saw "a Negro Woman with nothing on her but a very ragged Petticoat." William Attmore described the Tar River ferrymen as "ragged" in late December 1787, while one Revolutionary officer in 1781 commented in his journal that "their Negros tho' at this Season of the year [late November] are almost Naked in General. Some of them Quite as Naked as they were born have come into our Camp to look for pieces of Old Clothes." Children fared especially poorly in the distribution of ap-

Thomas Blount (1759–1812). Portrait attributed to Charles J. F. St. Memin, owned by the heirs of Lida T. Rodman. N.C. State Archives.

parel. Hazard saw "a Number of negro Children of both Sexes, stark naked today; they have never been clothed yet." Attmore saw a naked child in a tavern yard near Greenville in late December 1787, and five others near Washington who wore nothing but a shirt. The children at Thomas Blount's canal project went entirely bare, including the boy who waited on the white folks' table, and Scottish gentlewoman Janet Schaw was escorted through the streets of Wilmington "by a black wench half naked." Presumably, the slaves who suffered through the winter with no clothing at all were noteworthy for being unusual, but slave clothing in general was very scanty by the standards of eighteenth-century white observers.

Regardless of how well the slaves ate or how they lived or the difficulty of their tasks, the human relationship between slaves and masters was a difficult one. Slavery was based on compulsion and exploitation, a fact that eighteenth-century slaveowners accepted candidly. "It is the most disagreeable labour in the world," sighed Mrs. Ann Pettigrew, "that of making others work." No tales of loving black nursemaids or loyal family retainers appear in the letters of Mrs. Pettigrew, who was born into the Blount family and who married the plantation neighbor of Josiah Collins. Bonds of genuine mutual affection sometimes bridged the gap between master and slave, but nineteenth-century defenders of slavery tended to exaggerate such cases as part of their campaign to defend the South's "peculiar institution." Less sentimental than later generations, Mrs. Pettigrew and her husband realized that the slaves' obedience was never truly voluntary, and that a variety of measures was necessary to enforce the master's will.

Perhaps the most efficient methods were rewards for good work and the granting of privileges in recognition of superior talents or performance. Once these concessions had been given, the implicit threat of their removal could be an effective disciplinary measure. Common rewards were cash or prizes for extra work, permission to visit friends or relatives off the plantation, permission for a party or a religious service, or promotion to a position of skill or trust on the plantation. Most of the time, these positive incentives were sufficient, but the system of plantation discipline would have collapsed without the constant threat of punishments as well. When a slave's work was unsatisfactory to the master, he or she could be sold but this was not always convenient. The slave could not be fired, fined, or put in prison, for slaves were prisoners already. When a master believed that more punishment than the withdrawal of privileges was necessary, the simplest alternative was to inflict physical pain. The commonest tool for this purpose was the whip.

According to Charles William Jansen, "this instrument of punishment is made of the skin of an ox or cow, twisted hard when wet, and tapering off like a riding whip; it is hard and elastic, inflicting dreadful

wounds when used with severity." Jansen, an observer hostile to slavery, believed that whippings were common. "Often have I witnessed negroes dragged, without regard to age or sex, to the public whipping post, or tied up to the limb of a tree, at the will of the owner, and flogged with a cow-skin, without pity or remorse, til the ground beneath is dyed with the blood of the miserable sufferer." Other travelers slighted the subject of corporal punishment and focused on more casual forms of mistreatment like overwork, hunger, and cold. Some commentators, "Scotus Americanus" among them, insisted that North Carolina slavery was a benign institution. "Good usage is what alone can make the negroes well attached to their master's interest," he declared. "The inhabitants of Carolina, sensible of this, treat these valuable servants in an indulgent manner, and something like rational beings." The pamphleteer's slighting reference to slave rationality may betray his basic unreliability as an observer of blacks. Nevertheless, there were very few travelers who were in close contact with the most intimate details of plantation life, and a consistent account of slave punishments does not emerge from their writings.

A clearer picture appears in the writings of the slaveholders themselves. One case from the letters of the Pettigrew family is a good example of the human complexity of an institution that the law insisted was merely a property relationship.

The Reverend Charles Pettigrew (ca. 1744–1807) was an Episcopal minister of Edenton and vicinity who owned three plantations in the region of Albemarle Sound. Bonarva, the largest and most lucrative, bordered on the shores of Lake Phelps adjoining Somerset Plantation. Belgrade lay between Bonarva and Albemarle Sound, near the present town of Creswell, while Scotch Hall stood in Bertie County. Despite his extensive landholdings, the Reverend Mr. Pettigrew owned no more than about thirty-five slaves, which put him somewhat closer to the average North Carolina master than the owner of Somerset Place. Pettigrew's son Ebenezer inherited his father's property and expanded it by careful management and by his marriage to Ann Blount Shepard. The papers of father and son are a rich source of information on the daily reality of antebellum slavery in North Carolina.

Charles Pettigrew was not so different from other planters. He was a pious man who desired to be a kind master and a devoted Christian but who also wanted a productive plantation. He had been elected first bishop of the Diocese of North Carolina in the Protestant Episcopal church but failed twice to obtain proper consecration from another bishop. He finally abandoned the attempt when it became clear that religious duties would interfere with the profitable operations of his farms. He prayed for peace in Europe, but, when an upsurge of warfare sent the prices of his staple exports soaring, he could scarcely disguise his elation. Pettigrew's contradictory desires forced him frequently to acknowledge what he called "the difficulty of serving both God and mamon." The difficulty was nowhere more apparent than in Pettigrew's relations with his slaves.

The minister frequently complained that his slaves refused to work whenever his back was turned, but, as he explained to one correspondent, "we have no overseer, Choosing rather to oversee the negroes [ourselves], than an Overseer & them too." Pettigrew consequently relied on a set of trusted male slaves to supervise the work of the others. Among them were Fortune, who was in charge at Bonarva; Pompey, who normally lived at Belgrade but who shuttled frequently between the plantations; and Anthony, Cambridge, and George, who assisted at Belgrade.

The Pettigrews gave these men extra responsibility and depended on their cooperation, but they also viewed them with continual mistrust. "In regard to your wheat, I am afraid it is to[o] much exposed to the th[i]evishness of the negroes," Charles Pettigrew warned Ebenezer. "It is a very ready article of trade, & Fortune has his mercantile correspondents, who are ready at all times to receive him kindly." Hostility and dependency bred frustration on both sides of the racial chasm, a combination that flared into resistance by the

The Reverend Charles Pettigrew (1744–1807). Portrait by W. J. Williams, owned by Allen R. Pettigrew. N.C. State Archives.

slaves and violent retaliation by Pettigrew. As the minister remorsefully acknowledged, "to manage *negroes* without the exercise of too much passion, is next to an impossibility, after my strongest endeavors to the contrary, I found it so. I would therefore put you on your guard," he urged his sons, "lest their provocations should on some occasions transport you beyond the limits of decency and christian morality."

Most of the specific occasions when Pettigrew lost his temper are now lost to view, but one incident involving Pompey was probably typical. One Sunday morning in 1803, the aging minister directed his slave to accompany the family to church. Pompey objected, for this was not his regular job, but Pettigrew insisted because the other slaves were busy at their tasks. Pompey obeyed reluctantly, but Pettigrew did not ruffle the Sabbath calm with further reprimands. Early the next morning, Pettigrew "began to chide him for his behaviour on that occasion & he could not bear reproof." Angered, Pompey lashed back in self-defense; in the jargon of racial etiquette, he became "impudent" and suddenly the genteel man of the cloth was threatening his foreman with violence. Pompey stifled his rage a second time but he had evidently heard more than he could bear. During the confusion surrounding breakfast, the trusted foreman bolted for the woods.

No one knows now the pattern of indignities that somehow climaxed for Pompey when Pettigrew ordered him to church. He may have felt that driving the carriage and carrying the prayer books was too menial a job for the foreman, or he may have resented Christian proselytizing. He almost certainly had the customary right to a day off on Sunday. At all events, Pettigrew feared that Pompey's flight was no impetuous display of temper, but the result of a careful plan based on longstanding grievances. "I am afraid he has gone to Edenton," the minister wrote his son, "& perhaps intends trying to get to a Brother whom Cambridge boasts of having a white wife somewhere northward. . . . I am sorry, I had occasion to take him to Town lately, as he had opportunity to hear of so many getting off so easily from there." Knowing how much family ties meant to slaves, the elder Pettigrew warned Ebenezer to have Pompey's father in Edenton watched so that the fugitive might be captured with ease.

Pettigrew's fears were not fulfilled, for Pompey returned the following Sunday. Unwilling as always to violate the Sabbath, Pettigrew postponed Pompey's whipping until Monday, when he "made George give him a civil cheek for his impudence, & the loss of just a week's work." Stripped of his rank, Pompey was exiled to Bonarva to work under Fortune in disgrace.

In this complicated interchange, the whip was a last resort, the final symbol of Pettigrew's authority. The master preferred not to use it, but he did not hesitate when confronted with a challenge to his right of command. The power to inflict pain was essential to the sys-

Mary Blount Pettigrew (1750–86), first wife of Charles Pettigrew. Portrait by W. J. Williams, owned by Allen R. Pettigrew. Laura MacMillan, *N.C. Portrait Index, 1700–1860* (Chapel Hill, 1963).

The site of Bonarva Plantation is now within Pettigrew State Park, near Cresswell, Washington County. Only the white and slave cemeteries remain to be seen.

tem of slavery, and Pettigrew could not have operated his plantations without it.

In reflective moments, the well-meaning minister acknowledged reality bitterly. "It is a pity that agreeably to the nature of things, Slavory [sic] & Tyranny must go together—and that there is no such thing as having an obediant & useful Slave, without the painful exercise of undue & tyrannical authority." Violence was so crucial to eighteenth-century slave discipline that North Carolina's planter-dominated Assembly did not forbid the killing of slaves by masters until 1774. The murder of slaves by masters did not carry the same penalty as other murders until 1791, but even then the law did not apply to slaves who died as the result of "moderate correction."

Conscience-stricken, Charles Pettigrew could suddenly declare "I sincerely wish that there was not a Slave in the world," but he made no attempt to give up his power or to put his antislavery sentiments into practice. Many masters had none of Pettigrew's squeamishness. Conversing with William Attmore in 1787, Judge John Williams of Williamsboro "wished that there was an immediate addition of One hundred Thousand Slaves to the State . . . for the present ease and affluence," even though he admitted that the result might be a calamity for future generations. Not much given to such philosophizing, most North Carolina slaveowners accepted the world as they found it, enjoyed the material comforts that slaves produced, and dreaded the possibility that their slaves might rise against them in insurrection.

For the most part, North Carolina slaves resisted the power of their masters by individual and collective actions that made their condition more bearable but did not challenge the system of slavery as such. Bondsmen feigned sickness or ignorance, broke tools, stole food, sheltered runaways, and protected each other from the master's abuses. Slave families were a source of personal pride and mutual support for parents, children, and relatives alike. The slave community as a whole supported musicians, preachers, storytellers, healers, and craft workers who created a dynamic Afro-American culture that affirmed the human dignity of even the most persecuted inhabitant of the quarters. Weddings, funerals, religious services, and holiday celebrations gave slaves an opportunity to assert their humanity and their rightful equality with whites. When John Kooner gave orders every Christmas and Josiah Collins obeyed, the slave participants in the ritual had slyly claimed a moral right to change places with their owners. Opposition to slavery periodically went beyond foot-dragging on the job and cultural challenges in the quarters, but most acts of slave resistance were individual actions comparable to Pompey's brief flight from Belgrade.

Occasionally slave rebelliousness inspired more than individual resistance. In North Carolina as a whole, whites outnumbered blacks by two to one, and slaves were kept isolated on remote plantations, without the means of communicating plans or coordinating movements. It is therefore not surprising that slave insurrections were an uncommon occurrence. On at least two occasions, North Carolina slaves may have made an attempt to surmount these obstacles, although the evidence is ambiguous as in all such cases.

In 1775 the colony was rife with rumors that the British government would arm the slaves and send them against their masters in an attempt to halt the rapidly growing independence movement. The Pitt County Committee of Safety discovered what they called "a deep laid Horrid Tragick Plan laid for destroying the inhabitants of this province without respect of persons, age or sex." Forty slaves were arrested and at least ten received eighty lashes each and some others had their ears cut off. A large quantity of confiscated ammunition lent credence to the patriots' claim that they had nipped a major conspiracy just in time.

Almost two decades later, eastern North Carolina teemed again with rumors of slave conspiracies. Religious revivals and political controversy had unsettled community tranquillity in 1802, and a widely publicized conspiracy planned by Gabriel Prosser had been thwarted in Richmond, Virginia, only two years earlier. Influential whites claimed to have discovered written messages between groups of plotters up and down the Roanoke Valley, and many planters, including Charles Pettigrew and Thomas Blount, felt sure that their own slave households harbored some of the plotters. Retaliating instantly, courts in Bertie, Martin, Camden, Currituck, Perquimans, Hertford, Washington, Edgecombe, and Halifax counties hanged a total of twenty-one suspected participants and whipped and deported unknown numbers of others. Across the border in Virginia, two dozen other slaves lost their lives in the aftermath of the suspected uprising. Exaggerated white fears undoubtedly played a role in this and all other responses to the threat of slave rebellion, but white terror of black revenge was not entirely without foundation.

To Carolina slaveowners, the benefits of slave labor justified the risks that came with it. Historians have traditionally used the ownership of twenty slaves or more as an arbitrary cutoff point between the moderately prosperous farmer and the plantation owner. Whatever the size of their labor force, masters put their slaves to all kinds of labor, from plowing fields and sawing logs to cooking food and tending children. For the most part, slaves did work that would bring their owners the highest financial return, so they were especially active in producing goods for the export market. In the turpentine forests, slaves hacked and scraped the pine trees and chopped "boxes" in the trunks to catch the sap. When the juices stopped flowing in winter, slaves made tar and lumber or ventured into swamps to cut shingles and barrel staves. Some of the largest "plantations" in the

All the present courthouses in these counties date from a later period or have been extensively remodeled.

colony were actually more like logging camps. According to Janet Schaw, a Scottish lady who visited the lower Cape Fear in 1774, Mr. John Rutherfurd had a "vast number of Negroes employed in various works" at his Hunthill plantation on the Northeast Cape Fear River. "He makes a great deal of tar and turpentine," she wrote, "but his grand work is a saw-mill, the finest I ever met with." Skilled slaves made rafts and barrels for the products of Hunthill, and Rutherfurd was able to float 50,000 planks and one or two hundred barrels of naval stores to Wilmington every two weeks. "Everybody agrees," Miss Schaw noted admiringly, "that it [Hunthill] is able to draw from twelve to fifteen hundred [pounds] a year sterling money."

Cape Fear planters also grew rice along those narrow stretches of riverbank where fresh water rose and fell with the tide. They constructed elaborate dams and sluices to flood and drain their fields by tidal action. Rice cultivation was back-breaking work, for slaves were given hoes and sickles to cultivate and harvest the crop instead of more efficient plows and scythes. When they could be spared from the rice fields, slaves of these plantations grew indigo in the upland fields that could not be flooded. Indigo production ceased when the War for Independence put an end to the British subsidy, but rice and naval stores continued to be Cape Fear River staples until after the Civil War.

Farther inland, North Carolina planters grew the same kinds of crops their yeoman neighbors did, but in greater quantities. Even large planters wanted to be self-sufficient and tried to raise or make almost everything eaten or used on the plantation, but, much more than yeoman farmers, they counted on selling a large surplus every year as well. Backcountry plantations sold corn, wheat, peas, pork, beef, tobacco, flaxseed, and dairy products. Piedmont slaveholders were also likely to expand their operations with a sawmill, a gristmill, a tannery, or a store. The planter used these facilities himself and sought customers from the surrounding community as well.

Whether they owned one slave or dozens, North Carolina's slaveholders clearly had the chance to live more comfortably than the average small farmer. Just how much better they did live was something contemporaries disagreed about. Writing in 1773, an anonymous Scottish pamphleteer painted for prospective immigrants to North Carolina a glowing portrait of the life-style of colonial merchants and planters. "Their houses are elegant, their tables always plentifully covered and their entertainment sumptuous," declared "Scotus Americanus." "They are fond of company, living very sociable and neighbourly, visiting one another often. Poverty is almost an entire stranger among them, as the settlers are the most hospitable and charitable people that can be met with." The enthusiastic traveler could not find enough compliments to bestow on the leaders of the rapidly growing province, soon to be a colony no longer. "They are generous, well bred, and dress much; are polite, humane, and hospitable, and never tired of rendering strangers all the service in their power." All in all, the author concluded, Scotsmen dissatisfied with conditions at home could hardly do better than to come to North Carolina, where moderate efforts and slight expense could enable any hard-pressed farmer to share the life-style of such gentlemen.

At about the same time that "Scotus Americanus" was composing his glowing account, one of his countrywomen was forming a different opinion. "The people in town live decently," Janet Schaw admitted, "and tho' their houses are not spacious, they are in general very commodious and well-furnished." Once she left the homes of Wilmington merchants, however, Janet Schaw began to miss the elegance and good taste that "Scotus Americanus" had ascribed to plantation living. "There are two plantations on the banks [of the Northeast Cape Fear River]" she recalled, "both of which have the most delightful situations that is possible to imagine." If only the owners had the elementary sense of good taste to keep down the underbrush, she implied, they could perfect a magnificent landscape. "This however is too much for the listless hand of indolence and this beautiful place is overgrown with brambles and prickly pears, which render it entirely useless, tho' a few Negroes with their hoes could clear it in a week." What was worse, she observed, the stately mansion planned by one owner was abandoned half-finished "and he and his wife live in a hovel, while this handsome fabrick is daily falling

or Janet Schaw? Their two
er, the myth of Old South
provincial society with only
In a sense, both Scottish
us" described the ideal life-
oyed by a few, while Janet
ppeared between aspiration
stereotype was completely
f the oldest of the Piedmont
ation of planter families and

on a gentle hill in northern
vel fields stretch out toward
hich reaches in a wide bend
w a state historic site, the
it is easy to see why Philip
he came to the district in

lied the apparent tranquillity
River from Halifax County,
highly respected planters.

Tradition says that a Scot named McFadden built the House in the Horseshoe for Philip Alston. It also says that, after McFadden struck a white servant and found himself prosecuted for assault, he became disgusted with American notions of equality and returned to Scotland.

43

Like many families in the Albemarle and Roanoke regions, the Alstons had originally come from Virginia. Alston had married Temperance Smith, the heiress of a large tract of land on the Roanoke River, and Alston's father had given him slaves before he moved to the Piedmont. When old Mr. Alston died, he owned 150 slaves and 100,000 acres, but there was no further bequest for his son Philip. The young man had made unseemly haste to leave the Roanoke section because, some whispered, he sought to avoid a counterfeiting charge.

Philip Alston was not left without resources. Prior to 1777 he bought almost 7,000 acres of land in Cumberland County. He resold

The House in the Horseshoe (1772), Moore County, between Carbonton and Carthage.

much of this land, but in 1780, he still retained 2,500 acres, 20 slaves, 9 horses, 30 cattle, and £ 2,200 in cash. Alston was not only one of the two largest slaveholders in his district but the cash value of his taxable assets made him one of the wealthiest individuals as well. Alston was able to translate his economic position into political power. He was justice of the peace, member of the legislature, and colonel of the county militia.

During the American Revolution, Alston put his assertive nature at the service of his country. He commanded a band of soldiers against the actions of Tory guerrillas when they became active following British invasion of North Carolina in 1780. On one occasion, Alston's company captured an accomplice of the Tory officer David Fanning. They beat their prisoner with musket butts in an unsuccessful attempt to obtain information and then left him to die. Discovering the murder, Fanning swore revenge and ambushed Alston and his men at the House in the Horseshoe on 5 August 1781. After a fierce skirmish, Alston was forced to surrender and to promise not to fight the king's forces any longer. Bullet holes from this fight still scar the walls of Alston's home.

Bullet holes still clearly visible in the House in the Horseshoe walls.

After the Revolution, Moore County was split off from Cumberland and Alston served as its first clerk of court and later as state senator. When it was discovered that Alston stood indicted for the murder of yet another prisoner during the Revolutionary War and that he had denied the existence of God, the Senate expelled him from his seat, and he was later stripped of his post as justice of the peace. Governor Richard Caswell pardoned him for the murder. Soon thereafter, Alston tried to install his son as his successor in the post of Moore County clerk of court. A political rival who objected was soon discovered murdered on a night when the Alstons had been entertaining the neighborhood with a ball. Alston's slave Dave was charged with the crime, but Alston seems to have connived at Dave's escape. Jailed for contempt of court, Alston escaped and fled the state in 1790. He got as far as Georgia, where in 1791 an unknown assailant shot and killed him while he slept in bed.

Philip Alston was a powerful and violent man whose life and death exemplified the brutal aspects of frontier empire-building. The House in the Horseshoe was acquired in 1798 by Colonel Benjamin Williams, a man whose career bore some resemblance to Philip Alston's but whose character was remembered in a very different way by those who knew him.

Williams came from a planter family of Johnston County and married Elizabeth Jones of Halifax County. She was the daughter of a colonial official and half-sister of Willie and Allen Jones, both well-known Revolutionary leaders. Williams was a member of the First and Third Provincial Congresses and served under George Washington in the Continental Army, eventually reaching the rank of colonel.

Benjamin Williams (1754–1814). Portrait by an unknown artist, owned by the University of North Carolina. N.C. State Archives. His gravestone says more than his obituary about his character:

"Providence blessed him with a large share of its bounties and he acted as her faithful steward for large was his bounty and his soul sincere.
In his manners, with the open frankness of the soldier, was the dignity, and urbanity of the gentleman.
His hospitality and beneficence, in his several public and private relations gained him the respect and warmest attachment of all who knew him."

Widely respected and owning land in scattered counties, he was able to represent Craven, Johnston, and Moore counties in both houses of the General Assembly. His constituents sent him to the Third U.S. Congress (1793–95) but he did not seek reelection. To cap his political career, Williams received four one-year terms as governor of North Carolina in 1799, 1800, 1801, and 1807. He also sat on the board of trustees of the University of North Carolina from 1789 to 1802 and while governor acted as its chairman ex officio.

Benjamin Williams named the House in the Horseshoe "Retreat," and he used it initially as a country home and as an experimental cotton farm. The district was isolated, Williams complained, mail service was poor, and he did not particularly care for his neighbors. Later on, Williams moved to Deep River permanently and spent his last years there, raising cotton and training racehorses. He added wings to Alston's house (now removed), and he also built a granary, stable, weaving house, smokehouse, carriage house, and cotton house. The overseer and his family occupied a separate house, and nearby cabins sheltered the 103 slaves that Williams eventually acquired. When he considered the fertility of the land, the quality of the improvements, and the availability of more good land for purchase nearby, Williams could wax enthusiastic. "I think it may be justly ranked among the most valuable Estates in North Carolina," he announced to one potential purchaser, and declared its worth to be $30,000, a very sizable sum for 1803.

Plantation life agreed with Colonel Benjamin Williams. "I can assure you," he wrote to one friend, "with the little experience which has fallen my lot that in no pursuit have I yet found that enjoyment of contentment which agriculture affords." Nevertheless, planting carried its share of difficulties. Upland cotton had not been a profitable crop until Eli Whitney had discovered how to separate the fibers from the seed. Whitney had perfected his cotton gin in 1793, and while planters like Benjamin Williams were eager to try the new staple, they lacked experience in its cultivation. "In addition to my former Enquiries I beg leave to further trouble you on the Subject of the Culture of Cotton," he wrote to General William Henry Harrington. "How many Seed (when you plant in Hills) do you put in? Is it thought most advantageous to top and sucker Cotton & whether high or low should it be toped?" Williams also struggled against slaves and neighboring whites who tried to rob his fields at night, and he searched long and hard for a sober and competent overseer. When he finally secured the services of a certain Mr. Morrow, Williams called him "indeed a treasure, the best behaved man alive," but he worried about how he could continue to pay Morrow competitive wages. As an improving farmer, Williams experimented with mules instead of draft horses or oxen, but he found them hard to obtain. He complained about North Carolina's lack of good rivers or internal im-

Bedroom in the House in the Horse-shoe.

provements, and a bad experience with Fayetteville merchants led him to market his cotton directly in London. Williams was an enterprising country gentleman who obtained great wealth and extensive landholdings in North Carolina and the western states, but he never felt satisfied with the economic or cultural achievements of his native state.

Williams's personal letters show him to have been solicitous of his wife's health and of his son's education. He was fond of gracious living and the House in the Horseshoe frequently bulged with guests.

Williams's own description of the plantation in a letter to John Steele on 25 July 1803 gives a clear picture: "The River thro' these Lands forms the shape of an Horseshoe, leaving on the North side in a bend in the River about 1900 Acres, on which is a plantation of 454 Acres cleared . . . all of which except 50 Acres where the Houses are placed is first & second low ground under good fences & cross fences, a tolerable two story House with the frames now ready to put up a Wing of 24 by 20. at each end. . . . A Cotton House 60 by 20 feet pitch, long body, frame Roof, two range of floor divided by partitions proper for reception of & ginning of Cotton."

For several weeks in the summer of 1806, the old place sheltered five visiting relatives and one tutor, plus Colonel and Mrs. Williams and their son, Benjamin William Williams. By the time of his death in 1814, Williams had achieved a reputation as a model planter and ideal southern gentleman, for he was wealthy, hospitable, generous, public-spirited, conscientious, moderately progressive, an effective master, a devout Christian, a loving husband and father. The Raleigh *Minerva* honored his passing with a respectful tribute: "He died as he had lived, much respected and highly esteemed by those who knew him, and from his general demeanour and devout professions as well previous to as during his last illness, he has left his relations and more intimate friends the cheering consolation that he died a believer, resigned and happy in the hope of mercy through the atonement and merits of the Redeemer." Even when due allowances are made for eulogistic license, Benjamin Williams seems to have represented the best sort of man that his social class produced, just as Philip Alston may have represented the worst.

The wives of these two planters were both essential members of the plantation community. Little is known of Temperance Smith Alston except that she brought a large tract of land to her marriage, bore a large number of children, and negotiated the truce between her husband and David Fanning. Like Mrs. Alston, Elizabeth Jones Williams came from a distinguished family and no doubt contributed property to her husband's wealth. As plantation mistress, she probably supervised the work of slaves in the big house, the weaving house, and the kitchen. She had close contact with slave families and, as her will later revealed, developed special fondness for some of them, especially the women. Mrs. Williams's health was poor, however, and she may have lacked the strength for household tasks. She enjoyed the company of an intimate circle of female friends and relatives, but most of these women seem to have lived quite a distance from Deep River, some as far away as New Bern. Elizabeth Williams spent much of her time entertaining her friends and relatives as houseguests and paying extended visits to them in return, but she did not like to leave home without taking young Benjamin with her.

Elizabeth Williams survived her husband by three years and died in 1817 while visiting in New Bern. Her will lays open the web of close female and family relationships that composed her social world. Her son, Benjamin William Williams, inherited most of the property and served as executor along with William Martin, but Martin's wife Florah was entrusted with distributing personal bequests of clothing and other items. Two women witnessed the will, Laura Blake, who signed her name, and Sarah Taylor, who made her mark.

In a provision that Colonel Williams may have approved before his death, Mrs. Williams emancipated Essex, the trusted groom who had trained her husband's racehorses, and his wife Juno, as well as

Phebe, the wife of Arnold. Essex and Juno also received "one cow and calf, one sow and pigs and two ewes and lambs." The bulk of Mrs. Williams's "black cloths," which she had undoubtedly worn in mourning for her late husband, went to Juno, Phebe, Silva, and Hanna, with the remainder going to other slave women at Mrs. Martin's discretion. Certain other slaves were not freed but given to special friends, with careful attention to preserving family ties. Mrs. Ana Maria Littlejohn received Evelina and her two children, Lovelace, Evelina's brother, and Nanny and her child. John W. Guion of New Bern received two couples and their children, and one of the husbands' brothers. Simon was to be sold to a master of his own choice in Fayetteville, perhaps to reunite him with loved ones there, and Guion was to receive the money from the sale. It is impossible to know how these slaves felt about the arrangements made for them, or to know whether they reciprocated the feelings of affection that no doubt motivated Mrs. Williams. Individual manumissions tended to reinforce the slaveholders' sense of self-regard and were therefore ultimately self-serving, but it is also true that genuine feelings of mutual sympathy and respect could occasionally transcend the barriers between white and black. The other slaves of the Williams plantation remained in bondage.

The differences between the lives of Rachel Allen and Elizabeth Williams were striking. The pioneer's wife labored hard in her community, bore many children, and made an indispensable economic contribution to her household. For outside help, she drew on a dense network of friends and relatives in the immediate neighborhood, while she and her husband were partners in the myriad tasks of family survival. On the plantation, Elizabeth Williams doted on her only child, endured ill health, and spent her days in the restricted and conventional world that was the genteel woman's "place" in the nineteenth century. Her circle of female friends spread all over the state, but she had little to do with her close neighbors. Her husband was a soldier, politician, and man of the world. It was he who supervised the crops, chose an overseer, handled infractions of slave discipline, and even made the final decisions about his son's education. Planter and patriarch, Benjamin Williams necessarily exercised his authority with a firm hand, for final responsibility for making the coercive system of slavery work rested on him. As a slaveholder, Elizabeth Williams was a beneficiary of that system, but, as a woman, she was restricted by male-dominated society and thus victimized by it. Her will reflected this ambiguous social position. On the one hand, she did not disinherit her son or outrage public opinion and (perhaps) violate her own convictions by emancipating all her slaves. On the other hand, she had been free as a woman to develop the close emotional ties to slaves that were usually denied to white men. She shared her feelings with a tight circle of female friends and their web of shared relationships helped to mitigate some of the worst rigors of the system, though they did nothing to change its fundamental characteristics.

Like its two most famous owners, the House in the Horseshoe exemplified the extremes of plantation society. Its architectural details showed a close familiarity with the latest British fashion and its basic design and floor plan foreshadowed the most common house types and family living patterns of the nineteenth century. At the same time, the House in the Horseshoe is no lavish mansion. It is a plain, wooden, four-room house, with only a limited resemblance to the stately residences that contemporary landed magnates owned in tidewater Virginia or low country South Carolina. Planters like Benjamin Williams cherished high hopes for their estates, but their actual achievements were limited by substantial obstacles. Like the House in the Horseshoe, their homes revealed the fundamental simplicity of the world they really lived in.

Even when they were large, English houses of earlier centuries had been like the hall-and-parlor houses of coastal North Carolina. They tended to be asymmetrical; each room led directly into the other without the use of passageways, and they did not provide for much privacy or a specialized use of space. During the intellectual and artistic movement known as the Enlightenment, these features began to change. Ideas of order, balance, and symmetry became important aesthetic values in British culture. "Georgian" architecture, named for the three King Georges of the eighteenth century, reflected the popularity of these values. Built in 1770, Tryon Palace at New Bern was the outstanding example of Georgian architecture in the colony, but the House in the Horseshoe reflects Georgian principles in a domestic setting.

The Georgian style became very popular in America. The basic pattern of the House in the Horseshoe began to appear in many late eighteenth-century houses and was repeated endlessly in North Carolina farmhouses of the next century. Two rectangular rooms above, two beneath, a center hall on each floor, and a stairway in between—this was the simplest and cheapest way to arrange four rooms to make a broad and impressive exterior. The plan gave every moderately prosperous farmer a conspicuous symbol of respectability and status. Called the "central hallway I-house" by some architectural historians, because of its tall, thin profile, this type of dwelling has been called "perhaps the most common folk house type in the eastern United States." Long after classical Georgian architecture had come to seem outdated, the basic I-house floor plan with different stylistic embellishments persisted as the standard dwelling of the rural middle class.

Its popularity lay in its potential for the fulfillment of new ideals of family life and the separation of family life from work. Unlike earlier houses, each room in this dwelling had its own special function. The

50

dining room was on the left, the parlor on the right, and visitors waited in the hall until the family was ready to receive them. Cooking took place in the kitchen, a separate building in the rear. Sleeping, dressing, and bathing took place upstairs. There was one bedroom for parents and perhaps a baby; there was a separate room for the older children. The broad upstairs hallway belonged to everybody and was a good place for indoor work like spinning. Unlike the log cabin or the hall-and-parlor house, the spatial arrangement of the I-house seems recognizably modern.

The new house form mirrored and reinforced dramatic changes in the domestic life of the middle classes. In proper middle- and upper-class nineteenth-century households, work was something for servants and slaves, or for men to do away from home. This left the home increasingly a refuge for weary men and for women and children who, depending on one's point of view, were either trapped or sheltered in its confines. Parents relied less on the labor of their offspring, and modest progress against childhood diseases made it more likely that babies would live to maturity. Both of these developments encouraged parents to limit the size of their families. The reduced economic role of women elevated the importance of mutual affection as the basis of marriage. Among upper and middle classes, home became "sweet home," lovingly presided over by wives idealized as mothers and restricted to domestic duties. The outside world impinged less directly on the family, and a corresponding sense of privacy developed. A growing insistence on individual political rights seemed to find an echo in decisions to allocate private space to particular family members and to particular functions of the household. In the century to come, middle-class North Carolinians built fewer one-room cabins and hall-and-parlor houses, while the central hallway I-house spread across the landscape. As she sat with her only child in the tidy parlor of the House in the Horseshoe, Elizabeth Williams presided over a household that was the forerunner of a new kind of family, a changing set of values, and the slow but unmistakable emergence of a different kind of society.

Tryon Palace (1767–70), New Bern, Craven County. N.C. State Archives.

The Nimocks House (ca. 1804), Heritage Square, Fayetteville, Cumberland County, is thought to have been built by Duncan McCleran with shipwright labor. Shipping was of prime importance to this Cape Fear River port.

A visitor described Fayetteville in 1788: "Notwithstanding all which has been said against Fayette I think it by far one of the most agreeable towns in the State. I am sure it abounds more in all the good things of this World than the whole of the others put together. We have plays performed by the most eminent Actors for tragedy comedy etc. on an elegant Theatre. The wonders of the Magic Art are displayed in a most masterly manner by a little crooked leged fellow to the utter amazement of the gaping Yahoos." James Iredell Papers, 17 November 1788.

The same visitor teased his correspondent, "I would earnestly recommend to all the belles in Edenton District who are in want of husbands to come to this place. I will insure them at a very moderate rate that they shall not remain on hand more than three weeks the chance is excellent, there are several Rich old Batchelors who have very much a Consumptive appearance. Our Land lady is a good smart little woman enough but nothing uncommon she speaks Scotch Irish most divinely scolds like the devil is 25 Years of Age has dispatched two husbands already & is ready & looking out for a third." James Iredell Papers, 17 November 1788.

Towns in a Rural Society

"Places of wildness and rudeness, intemperance, ferocity, gaming, licentiousness, and malicious litigation!" President Joseph Caldwell of the University of North Carolina found the county seats of early nineteenth-century North Carolina tumultuous dens of iniquity, but not everyone agreed with him. Some travelers were more bored than shocked by the urban places of North Carolina. "The generality of towns are so inconsiderable," wrote J. F. D. Smyth, "that in England they would scarcely acquire the appellation of villages." Robert Hunter, Jr., felt equally unimpressed but spoke more bluntly. "Wilmington without exception is the most disagreeable sandy barren town I have visited on the continent," the young British merchant fumed in 1786. "I am extremely happy to think I shall leave it tomorrow." Even as the impatient traveler complained about North Carolina's second-largest town, he was forced to acknowledge the little port's significance to the state. "Several vessels are now lying in the harbor," Hunter recorded, "bound to the northward and different parts of Europe, laden with tobacco and naval stores." Hunter believed that the merchants of Wilmington exported three thousand hogsheads of tobacco annually; had he also estimated the traffic in naval stores he would have found an even larger volume of trade.

Out of a total population of less than two hundred thousand in 1770, there were fewer than five thousand North Carolinians who lived in places that might be called urban. Though they were all quite small, towns served North Carolina society as centers for government and trade. Every county courthouse attracted a collection of storekeepers, tavernkeepers, and artisans to serve the rural citizens as they transacted legal business. Moreover, even the most self-reliant pioneer could not make his own salt or iron, and few free families felt they could do without sugar, coffee, tea, or similar imported products. These articles could only come from stores, and a conveniently located store soon attracted enough business to form the basis for a hamlet. An inland settlement like the twin villages of Campbellton and Cross Creek (later united under the name Fayetteville) was the first stop in a journey that would carry plantation products to consumers around the world. An observer described the process. Storekeepers in Cross Creek bought backcountry products, he explained, and sent them down the Cape Fear River to Wilmington.

> These merchants, or the settlers along the river, make large rafts of timber . . . upon these they lay their beef, pork, and flower, in barrels, also their live stock, Indian corn, raw hides,

County seats attracted lawyers, who built offices in which to conduct their business. Because these were generally well-built, useful little structures, many have survived. Archibald Henderson's office (ca. 1800), Salisbury, Rowan County, became a schoolhouse and later a library. N.C. State Archives. Among many others that remain are William Gaston's office (before 1818), in New Bern, Craven County; and the Cameron-Nash Law Office (1801), in Hillsborough, Orange County.

Archibald Henderson wrote to William Gaston on 7 March 1810: "I am tired, seriously tired, of attending these County Superior Courts. Nothing but noise, confusion and ignorance. The profit is trifling, the Honor nothing."

Public accommodation in North Carolina was often cramped and dirty, with poor service and worse food. James Iredell wrote of his delight in finding something better in a letter to his wife on 12 March 1778: "We arrived at Hillsborough about one, found a most elegant tavern, dined with great satisfaction, and proceeded in the evening to a place about 10 miles further. Hillsborough rather exceeded my expectations; it is far from being a disagreeable town, as to appearance, and there is a remarkable handsome church in it."

Tavern rates were set by county courts. Here is a partial listing of charges set by Chatham court in August 1774:

A Hott Dinner with beer or Cyder   1/4
Cold Dinner   8p
Lodging in a good feather bed per
       night   4p
Pasturage per night for a horse   4p
Stablage with Foder or Hay per
       night   1/
West India Rum   hf. pt.   1/
New England Rum "   "   8p
Whiskey   "   "   6p
Bristol Beer per bottle   2/8
Madiera Wine per gallon   16/

(Right). Thomas Barker (1717–89) and Penelope Barker (1728–96). Portraits by John Wollaston, owned by the Cupola House Association. Courtesy Museum of Early Southern Decorative Arts.

(Right). The Barker House (ca. 1782), Edenton, Chowan County, restored and removed to the waterfront.

butter, tallow, and whatever they have for market. . . . The planters dispose of their goods to merchants in town, or to ships at Wilmington, where there are many now from Britain, the West Indies, and the different colonies; to these they sell their goods, and in return, bring back sugar, rum, salt, iron, &c. and the rest in cash.

Settlers were unwilling to live in the backcountry without occasional purchases from the outside world. For the planter who planned his whole year's work with the expectation of selling staple crops, market towns were clearly central to every economic activity. Though few in number, North Carolina's townsmen were crucial to the rural way of life.

Commerce called the towns into existence, but the little settlements meant far more to the average country family than sites for buying and selling, or even for carrying out legal business in the courts. Elections were held in towns and so were meetings of the assembly. Militia members gathered in towns to drill, and the congregations of the established church worshiped there. Taverns abounded in every town from the tiniest hamlet to the busiest seaport, and ranged in quality from filthy dramshops to elegant hostelries for gentlemen. Entertainment in the towns was a welcome relief from the monotony of rural life, and the typical visit to a town became the occasion for cutting loose from the restraints of ordinary existence. In a variety of ways, moreover, the pleasures that North Carolinians sought in towns were reflections of the same concerns, hopes, and fears that arose out of their work and their less dramatic daily lives. The chance for a drink, a hand of cards, or even an eye-gouging fight was a source of excitement that few pioneers would pass up. The popularity of these entertainments probably said more about the character of North Carolina society than President Caldwell would have preferred to admit.

The most influential and conspicuous townsmen were merchants. When he left Edenton in 1786, Robert Hunter, Jr., thought that "the people are almost all merchants here," but, as a literal statement of fact, that was far from true. Instead, most of the people depended on a relatively small number of merchants for their livelihood, and these merchants dominated the port both economically and politically. The home of Thomas Barker (1713–87), now on Edenton's waterfront, reflected the wealth and standing of this class of eighteenth-century townsmen. Men like Barker owned stores, warehouses, sailing vessels, and often plantations as well. They controlled town politics, and, by close association with the governor and the assembly, won high office in colonial and state government as well. Thomas Barker, for example, served as North Carolina's colonial agent to Great Britain shortly before the Revolution, a post that gave

The Iredell House (1778), Edenton, Chowan County. The long wing with the piazzas is a later addition.

him responsibilities somewhat comparable to those of an ambassador to the mother country. Barker also acted as justice of the peace in Bertie County; assemblyman for Edenton, Bertie County, and Chowan County; colonial treasurer; and collector of customs for Port Roanoke.

Towns were administrative and political centers, and the men who controlled these urban functions were also very important residents. Attorneys, judges, and royal officials maintained their homes and offices in the seaports, while a few other public servants lived in the smaller county seats. English-born James Iredell (1751–99) came to Edenton as deputy collector of the royal customs in the decade prior to the American Revolution. Iredell became a distinguished lawyer who sided with his adopted country in the contest for independence and who later sat on the United States Supreme Court. Iredell married Hannah Johnston (1747–1826), the niece of a former royal governor who brought to her husband a large fortune in land and slaves. Begun about 1773 by an earlier owner, the Iredells' house on East Church Street in Edenton was a monument to Iredell's personal success as well as a symbol of the close association between leading townsmen and powerful families in the country.

The Iredell-Johnston match was not unusual, for all segments of the colonial elite had the opportunity for similar personal ties. The principal lawyers and government officials were the merchants' close associates, for they protected business property in the courts and often asked businessmen to fill key posts in government. The merchants and lawyers together kept close ties to the largest planters, their principal customers and clients. Throughout the colonial period, merchants, lawyers, and planters held most of the seats in the Assembly, most of the appointive posts in colonial government, and managed the trade of the province. Where the established Anglican church had gained a foothold, these gentlemen sat on the parish vestry and regulated the religious life of the neighborhood. If there were a school in the vicinity, they served on the board of trustees and their children composed most of the student body. Their families mingled freely with one another and frequently intermarried. Planters' sons who tired of the country sought training as merchants and lawyers, while wealthy townsmen plowed profits into the purchase of land and slaves in the countryside. In the cases of some gentry families, urban and rural activities were so deeply intertwined that it sometimes became difficult to say where planting ended and commerce or politics began. In the closing decades of the eighteenth century, the planters and leading townsmen of eastern North Carolina comprised a unified elite that controlled the economy as well as the government of the province and to a lesser extent, dominated its religious and cultural life as well.

Not all urban residents enjoyed the wealth or comforts of Thomas Barker and James Iredell. The towns contained a middle class of smaller merchants and artisans who crafted articles like shoes, clothing, furniture, and houses for the other inhabitants; and barrels, boats, wagons, and wheels for the commercial traffic. Doctors, teachers, printers, and ministers found employment in the towns and so did unskilled laborers. "The poorest set of people whom I saw there," reported one admiring traveler, "are such as ply as sailers, or watermen rather on boats and lighters, up and down the rivers." These men led hard lives, and the pamphleteer thought they tended to ease their troubles with too much strong drink, but their presence was essential to the smooth operation of North Carolina's commerce.

Urban merchants had no intention of admitting the laboring classes—drunk or sober—to equal political rights in North Carolina's towns. In 1772 the leading gentlemen of Campbellton complained of an excess of democracy in town elections. "The men of property are the fewest in Number," they explained to the royal governor, "which must ever throw the power of determining the Election in the Hands of transient persons, Boatmen, Waggoners and other Laborers, and to take it from their Employers, who are principally interested in

James Iredell wrote in his proposal of marriage (1772) to Hannah Johnston, "It is not perhaps very becoming in a young man with so scanty an Income as I have to offer his hand and Heart for a young Lady's Acceptance—I rely Madam, upon your Goodness for an excuse of this Impropriety."

The tiny Birthplace of Andrew Johnson (ca. 1795), Mordecai Historic Park, Raleigh, Wake County.

securing or improving from their right of Representation, the property of the Town." The merchants petitioned Governor Martin for a property limitation on the right to vote, and the king's representative lost no time in granting their request.

The Andrew Johnson Birthplace in Raleigh is one of the few surviving houses associated with the poorer class of North Carolina townsmen. Measuring eighteen feet long by twelve feet wide, the tiny cottage stood for many years in the courtyard of Peter Casso's Inn, which opened in 1795 as one of the first hotels in Raleigh. Its cramped quarters and the overhead loft are reminiscent of the frontier log cabin though, like most urban structures, the Johnson house was made of sawn lumber. Jacob and Mary McDonough Johnson, parents of the seventeenth president of the United States, lived in the house with their two sons while he labored as hotel porter and she worked as a serving woman indoors at the inn. Lacking the independence of rural yeomen, the Johnsons were subject to their employer's call night and day.

Jacob Johnson died in 1812, when young Andrew was only three years old. Mrs. Johnson took up weaving on a hand loom to support herself and her children. She could not send the boys to school, but, when they reached their teens, she bound them to a tailor to learn the trade of making clothes. Unlike most other apprentices, Andrew Johnson escaped from the status of an artisan by a timely flight to Tennessee, where he married, learned to write, became a lawyer, and entered politics. Few North Carolina workingmen could even approximate this urban equivalent of the log-cabin-to-White-House success story.

Many urban residents were slaves who lacked even the minimal rights of the Johnson family. According to the U.S. Census, Edenton in 1790 contained 600 whites, 34 free blacks, and 941 slaves. Edenton's population seems to have been almost two-thirds black, but the statistics may include many plantation slaves whose owners lived in town. Fayetteville's population in the same year was more than one-third slave. Black men and women worked as house servants for the whites and as laborers, teamsters, and craftsmen in the town's commercial economy. Town slaves sometimes lived separately from their masters and could not be supervised as closely as the slaves on the plantation. Whites consequently feared them even more than slaves who were confined to the plantation. Ebenezer Pettigrew urged that the Edenton town guard be kept strong, for "the negros are two [sic] numerous there to have uncurbed liberty at night, night is their day" and warned his town-dwelling friends against complacency. White residents shared his worries, and subjected all blacks, both slave and free, to a dense array of special rules and prohibitions that were designed to prevent conspiracy.

The size and functions of towns could vary considerably according to the section of the state. "Towns we have none," wrote an anonymous resident of Moore County in the eastern Piedmont. "Fagensville [now called Carthage] a village at the Court House containing 8 or 10 dwelling Houses is the only place that claims a title to the name." Milton, located in Caswell County some eighty-five miles to the north, was not much larger. "Situated in the fork of Country-line [Creek] and Dan-river, it has 2 stores, a Saddler's shop, a Hatter's Shop, a tavern with about 15 or 20 houses," wrote Bartlett Yancey. The two pithy descriptions summarized much that could apply to the inland villages of the state: they were quite small; they came into existence around a courthouse or a juncture of transportation routes; and the principal inhabitants were storekeepers, tavern operators, and artisans.

One backcountry town that seemed exceptional was nevertheless like the others in the role it played within the region. Salem was the central, or congregation, town of the Moravian settlement at Wachovia. The Moravians, also known as the Unitas Fratrum or Unity of Brethren, were German followers of the early Protestant martyr Jan Hus. They came to America to establish an ideal Christian community in the wilderness. Moving from Georgia to Pennsylvania to North Carolina, they purchased close to a hundred thousand acres of prime Piedmont land from Lord Granville in 1753 and began to establish the settlement called Wachovia that same year. Their first town was a farming village named Bethabara, and Bethania soon joined it. By 1766 the agricultural operations were fully established and the Moravians agreed to build a third town, "not designed for farmers," as they put it, "but for those with trades."

The Brethren called the new town "Salem," a Hebrew word that means "peace." They built the community to reflect their conception of the Christian way of life and to express their central European ideas of orderliness and compact planned development. In the beginning, property in Salem was held in common. Individual families leased house lots on a yearly basis, but most of the town's trades and businesses were controlled by the community, acting through the church. The central town square, surrounded by church, schools, and other public buildings, conveys the sense of communal planning eloquently, as the congregation strove to reproduce the solidarity of a German village. Communal organization touched individual lives as well as the town's economy. Strong traditions of education and congregational music bound the generations to each other and fostered a sense of their collective identity. Moravians grouped themselves into "choirs" according to age, sex, and marital status. Children lived with their parents until the age of twelve, when they were apprenticed to learn a trade. Apprentices usually lived with their masters until they reached eighteen and lived thereafter with members of their choir, in the Single Brothers' House or the Single Sisters' House.

Salem Academy (1805), Forsyth County, started in 1772 and became a boarding school in 1802 because of the demand for female education by parents all over the state. The boarding school began with twenty girls and one teacher. This old drawing shows the structure before additions were made. Courtesy Old Salem Restoration.

Today, demonstrations of many trades take place daily in the Single Brothers' House at Old Salem, while the nearby Winkler Bakery gives visitors an opportunity to see, smell, and taste the products of skilled Moravian bakers.

The Saal [hall] of the Single Brothers' House (1769–86) was used for daily religious services. Single men and boys lived and worked in the house, each boy apprenticed to an artisan as economic demand dictated. Courtesy Old Salem Restoration.

The skills acquired by Salem youngsters distinguished the town from the rough-and-ready society of the frontier. "Every man follows some occupation," marveled one visitor in 1790. "Every woman is engaged in some feminine work; a tanner, shoemaker, potter, saddler, tinner, brewer, distiller, etc., is here seen at work; from their labors, they not only supply themselves but the country all around them." Eighteenth-century travelers unfailingly praised the display of frugality, neatness, hard work, and skilled workmanship they found among the Salem inhabitants. The Moravians, wrote one traveler, "live in brotherly love and set a laudable example of industry, unfortunately too little observed and followed in this part of the country." Elkanah Watson of Massachusetts agreed. "The moment I touched the boundary of the Moravians, I noted a marked and most favorable change in the appearance of buildings and farms," he wrote. "Even the cattle seemed larger, and in better condition. Here, in combined and well-directed effort, all put shoulders to the wheel, which apparently moves on oily springs."

Elkanah Watson (1758–1842). N.C. State Archives.

The Salem potter, Brother Aust, in 1773 had the luck to hire a journeyman potter from the English Wedgwood factory and learned from him the techniques of making queensware, a high-fired, cream-colored earthenware of rococo design. This gave Moravian pottery an excellence unmatched in the colonies at that time.

Examples of Moravian pottery may be seen in the Krause-Butner Potter's House in Bethabara, Forsyth County.

Miksch Tobacco Shop, Old Salem. On the shelves are wound ropes of tobacco, from which lengths or "twists" were sold. Courtesy Old Salem Restoration.

Moravian craftsmanship attracted a steady stream of customers to Salem. J. F. D. Smyth took particular notice of "a very extensive [manufactory] of earthenware, which they have brought to great perfection, and supply the whole country with it for some hundred miles around." In Salem itself, the Market-Fire House on the town square was the focal point of buying and selling of Moravian products, while the Miksch Tobacco Shop is a further example of Moravian commercial architecture and life-style. Like most of the families in Salem, the Miksch household conducted their business on the ground floor and used the upper story for living space. Many of the customers at the tobacco shop came from several days' journey away,

Salem Tavern (1784), the gentlemen's room. Courtesy Old Salem Restoration. George Washington stayed at the tavern when he visited Salem in 1791. He wrote in his diary: "Salem is a small but neat village; and like all the rest of the Moravian settlements, is governed by an excellent police—having within itself all kinds of artisans. The number of Souls does not exceed 200." On 1 June he "spent the forenoon in visiting the Shops of the different Tradesmen, the houses of accommodation for the single men and Sisters of the Fraternity, and their place of worship. Invited six of their principal people to dine with me and in the evening went to hear them sing, and perform on a variety of instruments Church music." The Salem Diary tells the rest: "At the close of the day the wind instruments were heard sweetly beside the Tavern." Fries, ed., *Records of the Moravians*, vol. 5.

and stopped there as part of an extended shopping trip for manufactured products. Hundreds of these Piedmont farmers camped by the roadside as they traveled; others pampered themselves at the well-appointed Salem Tavern, which adjoined the town square. President George Washington was only one of many distinguished tourists who found an evening's shelter in the tavern's comfortable chambers.

Organized, disciplined, and highly trained in specific crafts, the Salem Brethren lived very differently from the more individualistic pioneer farmers and jacks-of-all-trades who surrounded them. The Moravians and the backcountrymen nevertheless needed each other. Salem was a market for all varieties of country produce, and Moravian teamsters made regular trips to Cross Creek and other fall-line towns to dispose of surplus commodities like corn and flour. In return, Salem supplied the backcountry with all varieties of manufactured products and also served as a distribution point for imports like sugar, coffee, tea, and salt. Salem's community organization was unique, as were the high standards of workmanship and the appearance of the town itself, but the position it held in the backcountry was not unlike the role performed by Hillsborough, Salisbury, Charlotte, and the smaller Piedmont villages.

When the Moravian storekeeper measured out English yard goods to a Stokes County customer, he was acting as the last link in a chain of buyers and sellers that relayed foreign manufactures westward across the Atlantic. When the customer paid for his cloth with a load of flour or country ham, he was starting a flow of transactions in the opposite direction that would send American products across the ocean to repay the English manufacturer. The next step in this steady stream of business typically took place in a town farther east, where a sudden drop in elevation put waterfalls and rapids in the way of farther upstream navigation. Towns sprang up at the "fall line," where coastal shippers transferred their freight from river craft to covered wagons and countrymen did the reverse.

The Moravians ordinarily hauled their customers' products to Cross Creek, at the head of navigation on the Cape Fear River. Cross Creek grew up beside a gristmill site about a mile from the river itself; Campbellton was the village that actually bordered on

An inventory of Salem Tavern taken in 1807 shows 17 double featherbeds, 17 double chaff beds, 10 blankets, 17 woolen counterpanes, 17 cotton counterpanes, 65 bed sheets, 35 towels, 25 tablecloths, rafts of pillows and pillowcases, 17 double bedsteads, and 60 chairs. Fries, ed., *Records of the Moravians*, vol. 6.

Salem Tavern, the Ordinary Room. Courtesy Old Salem Restoration.

the waterfront. As the two towns grew together, they adopted a common government and assumed the name Fayetteville in 1783 in honor of the Marquis de Lafayette. The merchants who accepted the Moravians' shipments loaded the pork, flour, butter, hides, tallow, flaxseed, beeswax, and tobacco onto rafts and floated them to Wilmington. Returning homeward, the flatboat crews poled up heavy loads of foreign imports for Moravians and other storekeepers to retail through the backcountry. Cross Creek was the largest of these midland North Carolina towns but it was by no means alone. Halifax and Tarboro served similar functions, as did Kinston and Lumberton on a smaller scale.

Tarboro was the embarkation point for tobacco raised by planters throughout the upper portion of the Coastal Plain. After packing his leaf in a hogshead, the farmer passed an axle through the center, hitched a team to the huge cask, and rolled his crop directly to market on the country roads. After visiting the inspector at Tarboro, the planter deposited his tobacco in exchange for a warehouse receipt, which he could then sell for cash or store goods from one of several village merchants. The tobacco business made Tarboro an important place, and the legislature chose to meet there on occasion. "The Town contains about twenty Families, and for the size of it has a considerable Trade," William Attmore reported. "It is situated on a high flat piece of Ground, and is a very pleasant place." Thomas Blount (1759–1812) took advantage of Tarboro's location and put one of his family's principal stores and warehouses there. He also served as town commissioner, justice of the peace, assemblyman, trustee of the University of North Carolina, and U.S. congressman. The Blount-Bridgers House in Tarboro is a reminder of his contribution to Tarboro's past.

Of all the eighteenth-century trading centers on North Carolina's inland rivers, Halifax is the best preserved today. J. F. D. Smyth visited the little port in the 1770s and described it very favorably. "Halifax is a pretty town on the south side of the Roanoke," Smyth told his readers. "About eight miles below the first falls, and near fifty miles higher up than the tide flows, but sloops, schooners, and flats, or lighters, of great burden, come up to this town against the stream, which is deep and gentle. Halifax enjoys a tolerable share of commerce in tobacco, pork, butter, flour, and some tar, turpentine, skins, furs, and cotton," Smyth continued. "There are many handsome buildings in Halifax and vicinity, but they are almost all constructed of timber, and painted white."

Founded in 1757 as a commercial venture, Halifax boasted some sixty houses twelve years later. President George Washington thought the population was less than a thousand when he came through in 1791. When the railroad bypassed the town after 1839, Halifax dwindled in size, but during the late eighteenth century, it

Washington commented as follows on Tarboro: "This place is less than Halifax, but more lively and thriving. . . . Greenville is on Tar River and the exports the same as from Tarborough with a greater proportion of Tar—for the lower down the greater number of Tar makers are there—This article is contrary to all ideas one could entertain on the subject, rolled as Tobacco by an axis which goes through both heads—one horse draws two barrels in this manner." George Washington, *Diaries*.

The Blount-Bridgers House (1808), St. Andrew St., Tarboro, Edgecombe County, is being restored for use as a community center and art gallery.

64

Constitution-Burgess House.

was the center of trade and government for the entire Roanoke River Valley. The Fourth Provincial Congress assembled there in 1776 and recommended that North Carolina join with the other colonies to declare independence. Nine months later, the Fifth Provincial Congress met in Halifax and adopted North Carolina's first state constitution. The little town was a county seat, the center of a judicial district, and one of the few towns guaranteed a seat in the legislature by the 1776 constitution.

Market Square was the center of activity when Halifax was in its heyday. A three-day market fair was held there annually in the last two decades of the eighteenth century. The square was also the spot for militia drill, election rallies, playing, promenading, and grazing livestock. As in Tarboro, an official state tobacco warehouse and inspection station stood nearby. Legal business could be taken care of at the courthouse or at the law office of one of Halifax's several resident attorneys. The Constitution-Burgess House has been furnished as the town house and office of Thomas Burgess, a lawyer of the early nineteenth century. Business completed, planters from the rich plantation district up and down the river gathered to socialize with their peers at the Eagle Tavern, which J. F. D. Smyth called

The Eagle Tavern (1790s), once a part of the Eagle Hotel complex, but not the oldest Eagle Tavern (1770s), has been restored to its original exterior form.

"This place [Halifax] contains about 50 houses, stores are kept here to supply the country round with European and West India Commoditys for which Pork, Tobacco, Indian corn, Wheat and Lumber are taken in return." *Journal Kept by Hugh Finlay, 1773–74.*

The Owens House (1760), Halifax, Halifax County, now relocated and restored as a merchant's house of the early nineteenth century.

"the best house of public entertainment in Halifax." Alternatively, they could try out the facilities of a smaller ordinary, now called the "Tap Room." When this very early (1762) town house became part of "Pope's Hotel," it contained the only public billiard table in the community.

The families who made Halifax their permanent home had come to the Roanoke Valley from Virginia and from the older settled regions around Albemarle Sound. They brought housing styles from the east with them. The Owens House in Halifax is a merchant's dwelling that reflects the builder's place of origin. The gambrel roof was popular all over eastern North Carolina in the eighteenth century; it may have originated as a device for building a two-story house that required the tax payments of only a one-story structure. The side-hall plan of this house originated in the Albemarle area, and clearly separates the parts of the house according to family function.

One downstairs room is furnished as a family parlor, the other as the merchant's office. Upstairs, two bedrooms are for the merchant's family, the other for his clerk. The kitchen is in the rear. This late eighteenth-century urban family was able to keep its private life separate from business, and preferred to do so.

Inland traders who carried on the commerce of towns like Halifax, Tarboro, and Cross Creek shipped the backcountry staples onward to seaport towns like Edenton, Washington, New Bern, and Wilmington. Throughout the late eighteenth and early nineteenth centuries, these towns were the largest and most imposing in North Carolina. Here lived the largest merchants, the royal officials, and the lawyers and judges who dominated all of colonial and early federal society and government. These gentlemen saw to it that North Carolina's port towns, though small, were more comfortable and attractive than any other settlements in the state. "Edenton was the first town we came to in North Carolina," wrote German traveler Johann David Schöpf, "and it is none of the worst, although consisting of not more than 100 framed houses, all standing apart and surrounded with galleries or piazzas." The galleries were tropical innovations, introduced from the West Indies as a means to escape the heat. The Barker family used a two-story piazza running the full length of their house to catch the evening breezes off the sound, and most of their affluent fellow townsmen did likewise.

The same Englishman who detested Wilmington agreed that Edenton was much more agreeable to the visitor. "They reckon about 1,000 to 1,500 inhabitants in Edenton," Robert Hunter reported. "The town is laid out in the form of a square, built on the Albemarle Sound, which is to the southward. . . . They have here a tolerable good brick statehouse, a brick church, and a market place from whence they are supplied every day." Many of the stately public buildings that graced Edenton when Hunter arrived in 1786 are still standing. The "good brick statehouse" was the Chowan County Courthouse (1767), which has been called "perhaps the finest Georgian courthouse in the South." Like the courthouse, the brick St. Paul's Episcopal Church (1736–74) is still in active use, as are many of the wooden homes of merchants and officials whom Hunter would have been able to visit.

Charles Biddle, a Philadelphian who lived in North Carolina during the Revolution and represented Carteret County in the General Assembly, later wrote of his experience: "Being naturally active . . . sitting so long as we did in the Legislature was a most disagreeable thing to me, and what made it much more so than it otherwise would have been, was the frequent disputes between the members from the western and those from the eastern parts of the State. This I believe to be the case in all the States of the Union. Those from the westward look upon people in any of the commercial towns as little better than swindlers; while those of the east consider the western members as a pack of savages. In their debates, instead of using the language of persuasion, which should always be done in the Legislature, they were continually abusing each other."

In 1777 Ebenezer Hazard attended a Christmas Day service at St. Paul's. "Heard Mr. Earl preach in the Church. . . . The Parson's Notes were very yellow & the last Leaf loose from which I conjecture they were rather ancient & had been much used." Hazard's innkeeper entertained his guests gratis that day, giving them among other things "Arrack Punch and Venison."

Sketch of Wilmington, New Hanover County, by Hugh Finlay at the time of his postal-route reconnaissance, 1773–74.

William Attmore described New Bern's houses: "There are to many of the houses Balconies or Piazzas in front and sometimes back of the house, this Method of Building is found convenient on account of the great Summer Heats here—These Balconies are often two Stories high, sometimes one or both ends of it are boarded up and made into a room."

Francis Asbury described his visit to New Bern in 1802: "Newbern is a trading and growing town; there are seven hundred or a thousand houses already built, and the number is yearly increased by less or greater additions, among which are some respectable brick edifices; the new courthouse, truly so; neat and elegant. . . . The population of the town, citizens and transient persons, may amount to three thousand five hundred or four thousand Souls."

Attmore noted the public buildings too: "There is a small church here with a square tower, Cupola and Bell & it is the only place of Worship in the Town. This place being the County Town of Craven County, there is a brick Gaol here and a Court House, the latter raised on Arches; the Courts being held upstairs, the lower part serves for a market place."

Edenton and Wilmington were important commercial centers and both had their defenders as the most attractive or wealthiest port in North Carolina, but the town that exceeded them both in size and significance was New Bern. Located in Craven County where the Neuse and Trent rivers came together in a broad estuary leading toward Pamlico Sound and Ocracoke Inlet, New Bern had been founded in 1710 by Baron Christoph von Graffenried, a Swiss nobleman who sought to create a place of refuge for the Protestant victims of Swiss and German wars. After Bath, New Bern was the second oldest town in the province. The baron's settlement had been virtually wiped out by the Tuscarora Indians in 1711, but the location, halfway between the flourishing settlements in the Albemarle and the Cape Fear sections, was advantageous to commerce. After the defeat of the Tuscaroras, the Neuse River Valley continued to grow and became an important center of population in its own right.

New Bern remained small until after mid-century, but its central location made it increasingly popular as a meeting place for the colonial assembly. When William Tryon became royal governor in 1765, he quickly asked the Assembly to make it the permanent capital of North Carolina and to appropriate funds for the construction of a building to contain government offices, assembly and council chambers, and a residence for the governor and his family. The result was Tryon's Palace, an architectural gem that was the marvel of foreign visitors, the pride of the little capital, and an object of resentment for backcountry taxpayers. The economic burden of paying for Tryon's Palace contributed to the uprising of Regulators on the Piedmont frontier, but the economic benefits to New Bern were instantaneous. As soon as the town became North Carolina's seat of government, the number of licensed ordinaries or taverns shot up to 26 in anticipation of annual throngs of thirsty legislators. The steady stream of official visitors to courts and offices kept the innkeepers busy year round. Planters and merchants with court business found it convenient to combine commerce with politics and lawsuits, and the little seaport boomed. When Governor Josiah Martin took office in 1771, he reported back to London that New Bern had gathered the trade of Beaufort to itself and was "growing very fast into significance." If only the navigation difficulties that obstructed the channel leading to open ocean were removed, he speculated, "I do think it would then soon become a City not unworthy [of] notice in the great and flourishing Empire of my Royal Master." Growth accelerated in the decades following American independence, but New Bern never seriously rivaled the eminence of Charleston, South Carolina, or Chesapeake ports like Norfolk, Virginia, or Baltimore, Maryland. New Bern expanded from 150 houses and 1,000 persons in the mid-1770s to 400 houses and 2,000 persons in the 1790s. By 1800 New Bern was the largest town in the state, with 2,567 residents, as compared with

1,689 in Wilmington, 1,565 in Fayetteville, and 1,302 in Edenton.

Throughout the eighteenth century, merchants' wharves clustered along New Bern's Trent River shoreline. The public wharf of Craven County dominated the waterfront at the foot of Craven Street. Lumber and naval stores were the principal articles of commerce, but, as elsewhere in the state, tobacco and provisions were eagerly traded as well. West Indian vessels landed with sugar, salt, molasses, rum, and an occasional consignment of slaves. The number of vessels bound directly from Europe dropped off after the Revolution, but coastal vessels from Philadelphia, New York, and New England took their places. Processing industries sprang up in New Bern to further refine the commodities that traveled through the port. A tanyard prepared leather from the hides of backcountry livestock, and a distillery transformed West Indian molasses into rum. Elsewhere about town, artisans' and tradesmen's shops lined the streets. Coopers supplied the shippers with barrels to carry their products. Shipwrights repaired the sailing vessels and wheelwrights serviced vehicles from the country. Luxury blossomed from the skills of cabinetmakers, tailors, milliners, silversmiths, and even a wigmaker. Slaves, seamen, and flatboat crews jostled planters, lawyers, merchants, and sea captains in the streets, arousing a concern for municipal security. A statute of 1773 imposed the first tax for the purchase of a fire engine and a night watch and banned fast driving in the city streets. The lawmakers also noted that "sundry idle and disorderly Persons, as well as Slaves, and Children under age, do make a Practice of firing Guns and Pistols within the . . . Town," and prudently forbade such activity for the future. Little New Bern was a frontier village no longer.

Visitors to New Bern always noticed the impressive brick public buildings that contrasted with the wooden stores and dwellings of the inhabitants and with the rough-and-ready structures of the backcountry. Besides the palace, other public buildings were noteworthy to visitors. The county courthouse, raised on arches in a public square where the road from the Cape Fear entered New Bern, housed the offices of local government and shaded a public market twice a week. Country people with fresh produce could vend beneath the arches, but a commoner practice was to carry fish and vegetables in canoes to the waterfront and hawk one's wares along the docks. Not far from the courthouse at the intersection of Broad and New streets stood the old Anglican parish church. Graced with a square cupola, Christ Church for many years was the only building for public worship in New Bern. The graves of leading citizens fill its quiet churchyard, and more can be found in Cedar Grove Cemetery not far away.

Urban amusements unknown to frontier North Carolinians competed for patronage in the crowded lanes of the colonial capital.

Sketch of Christ Episcopal Church, New Bern, from the Jonathan Price map, ca. 1810, owned by O. Haywood Guion. N.C. State Archives. Nothing remains of the 1750 structure but some foundation stones in the corner of the churchyard. The present Christ Church dates from 1875.

THEATRE.

Friday

On ~~Thursday~~ evening the 19th instant, will be performed, the

TRAGEDY of

Venice Preserved.

Duke of Venice,	*Mr. Cook,*
Priuli,	*Mr. J. Norfleet,*
Bedamar,	*Mr. W. Skinner,*
Jaffier,	*Mr. Iredell,*
Pierre,	*Mr. Littlejohn,*
Renault,	*Mr. T. Norfleet,*
Elliott,	*Mr. Roberts,*
Spinosa,	*Mr. Moffatt,*
Theodore,	
Belvidera,	*Mr. T. Skinner.*

OFFICERS and SENATORS, by other Gentlemen of the Town.

To which will be added, the FARCE of

Raising the Wind.

Diddler,	*Mr. Cook,*
Fainwould,	*Mr. Iredell,*
Plainway,	*Mr. Littlejohn,*
Sam,	*Mr. M'Connel,*
Waiter and Richard,	*Mr. T. Skinner,*
Servant to Plainway,	*Mr. T. Norfleet,*
Miss L. Durable,	*Mr. W. Skinner,*
Peggy,	*Mr. Lowther.*

Mr. *Littlejohn* and Mr. *Cook* will perform a Recitation each, between the Tragedy and Farce.

Doors to be opened at half past 5, and curtain rise at half past 6 o'clock.

** TICKETS to be had at Mrs. Horniblow's, price 1 Dollar each—Children half price.

January 17, 1810.

Troupes of visiting players offered theatrical performances such as *Isabella, or the Fatal Marriage* and comic operas like *The Poor Soldier.* A theater was devised in the "still Room" of the molasses distillery that included a gallery for free black patrons. Townsmen enjoyed billiards, cards, music, horse races, and drinking in taverns. Gambling was a pastime that attracted every level of society. Much to his dismay, William Attmore found "white boys and negroes eagerly betting ½ a quart of Rum, a drink of Grog &c., as well as Gentlemen betting high" at one Saturday's horse race. More refined entertainment was available from the first bookseller to locate in North Carolina, and from the lessons being offered in drawing, music, dancing, and French by itinerant instructors.

An outstanding community celebration in New Bern graced the 1791 visit of President Washington. The festivities included a parade, a public dinner, and an exclusive ball in the palace. The wedding that year between Daniel Carthy and Sarah Hasler was, if anything, more lavish still. The ceremony was followed by tea, then by dancing and a "very elegant set supper" with two wedding cakes. Parties continued for four days thereafter, concluding with a shipboard "relish" for the gentlemen of the wedding party. Dainty confections for such a fete could be whipped together from the wares of a tropical fruit shop, one of the few places in North Carolina to stock oranges, pineapples, lemons, coconuts, and almonds on a regular basis. On more solemn occasions, affluent New Bernians marked funerals with white linen scarves and hat bands for the minister and the pallbearers. After the funeral, the linen was sufficient to make each man a new shirt. Even in death, a high level of consumption was expected of New Bern's leading families.

John Wright Stanly (1742–89) was a New Bern merchant who typified North Carolina's few urban elite. The topsy-turvy business conditions of the American Revolution and its aftermath lifted Stanly to the height of opulence and more than once dropped him almost as far in the other direction. Through all his vicissitudes, Stanly hung on to the personal connections and the business acumen that were the secret of his success, and in the end left a promising family whose members reestablished the family fortune and exercised substantial leadership in the independent state of North Carolina.

A lawyer's son from Amelia County, Virginia, Stanly was early thrown on his own resources by the death of his father and his mother's remarriage. After starting work as a merchant's clerk at the age of fourteen, Stanly followed the currents of British imperial commerce from Williamsburg to Nova Scotia to Jamaica. An allegation of association with counterfeiters followed Stanly from Williamsburg to Nova Scotia, but the eighteen-year-old youth was never prosecuted, and he later blamed ignorance and inexperience for any involvement he may have had with the misdeeds of others. Quarrels with a Phila-

(Left) A broadside for two plays presented at Edenton in 1810. The actors were a group of town gentlemen. Among them was James Iredell, Jr., who saved this bill among his papers.

Pitcher showing a Stanly privateer.
N.C. Museum of History Collection.
N.C. State Archives.

delphia partner landed him in the debtors' prison in that city until vindicated by the courts, but Stanly recouped his finances and regained the respect of Philadelphia's merchant community.

When he was thirty, a chance visit to North Carolina introduced John Wright Stanly to Ann Cogdell (1753–89), daughter of one of New Bern's leading families, and the footloose entrepreneur decided to marry her and settle down. After moving his business to New Bern, Stanly became what his eulogist later called "a merchant of the greatest enterprise and most extensive business ever known in this State." Success silenced all questions about the past, and Stanly took a prominent position as one of the state's most admired businessmen. His trade was so extensive that he maintained two homes, one in Philadelphia and one in New Bern, and his frequent visits to the northern metropolis kept him in regular contact with leading Revolutionary figures like Thomas Jefferson and Robert Morris, the financier.

A substantial part of John Wright Stanly's fortune derived from the Revolutionary War, when Stanly outfitted as many as fourteen privateering vessels in New Bern and Philadelphia and deployed his private navy to capture British prizes valued as high as £70,000. A cannon from H.M.S. *Lady Blessington* stands in the yard of Christ Church as a trophy of Stanly's privateering conquests. Stanly also lent large sums for the prosecution of the war and supplied American armies with weapons and provisions, for most of which he was never repaid.

Further reversals occurred when the British captured Stanly's fleet in the Caribbean and raiding Tories burned his wharves and warehouses. Struggling to recoup his fortunes once more, Stanly held on to his house in New Bern, his large wharf and distillery, his plantation, and his sixty slaves. New Bern's leading merchant staved off bankruptcy, but his finances had not fully recovered when a yellow fever epidemic swept over the town in 1789. John Wright Stanly and his wife were among its victims. Within a month of each other, they were buried side-by-side in the cemetery of Christ Church.

The most stable element of Stanly's fortune was his opulent mansion on the corner of Middle and New streets. Tradition identifies the architect as John Hawks, designer of Tryon's Palace itself. Like the palace, the Stanly House is in the Georgian style, but it displays many decorative features of country estates in the Hudson and Delaware river valleys of Stanly's New York and Philadelphia associates. The house has a hipped roof, two interior chimneys, a center hall on each of two floors, and four symmetrically arranged rooms downstairs and up. It is made entirely of wood with long pine timbers laid flush on the outside for a smooth appearance and carved at the corners to resemble quoins. The woodwork inside and out is richly carved and heavily decorated, "certainly the finest of the period in the state." Once a penniless clerk, John Wright Stanly had accumulated the fortune of a merchant prince, and he spent it in princely style.

Stanly's failures reflect the instability of mercantile wealth just as his successes show that skill, a fortunate marriage, and the right connections enabled the favored individual to weather temporary reverses. In Stanly's case, success counterbalanced failure and admitted him to the few elite that controlled the economy, society, and government of the new state. The position of the North Carolina elite was less exalted than their counterparts in Virginia and South Carolina. In contrast to those colonies, North Carolina's leading families had more recent origins, less sizable estates, and less social exclusivity. Stanly was fortunate in his selection of North Carolina as a permanent home, for it is unlikely that such a relatively unknown adventurer could have made a prestigious marriage or won such easy confidence among the elite of Charleston or the Chesapeake. By the same token, North Carolina's planters and merchants probably held a

The John Wright Stanly House (1780s), New Bern, Craven County, achieved an elegance foreign to the colony of North Carolina at that time. John Hawks was the probable architect. Courtesy Tryon Palace Restoration.

more slippery position at the top of their society than their counterparts elsewhere in the late colonial period. Some historians have suggested that the precarious position of the upper class made its members less scrupulous and more openly exploitative than they might otherwise have been, and thus more tolerant of those government abuses that finally provoked the Regulator uprising in the 1760s and early 1770s. The relative openness of North Carolina's elite did not necessarily make the society more democratic or more just.

Recurrent incidents in Stanly's career suggest that the route to success might involve pushing beyond the limits of what was legal or honorable to exploit a favorable opportunity. There was the counterfeiting charge, the prison sentence, and lingering hints of improper actions. When Stanly first applied for a privateer's license, for example, William Tisdale of the New Bern Committee of Safety testified to Stanly's patriotism in a letter of praise and commendation. Weeks later, however, Tisdale lamented his earlier recommendation: "I am sorry to say that since the writing of the s'd letter, I have been inform'd of several Circumstances in the Conduct of the afores'd gentleman which puts me under the disagreeable necessity of desiring you to look upon that letter as tho' it was never wrote." Nonetheless, Stanly obtained his license to plunder British shipping.

Members of the transatlantic trading community, like Stanly, lived by a code that required rigid punctuality in the fulfillment of contracts and a vigorous pursuit of their own interests within the stipulations of any agreement. In his will, Stanly proudly insisted that "my debts be honestly paid, I mean in such kind of money as I agreed to pay when I contracted them, and not depreciated paper for Gold and Silver." No merchant could long survive without personal independence and a reputation for reliability, but they were not the only men who prized these qualities. Lawyers, planters, and other members of the elite guarded their reputations for the same reasons. Lawyers lived in a world of courtroom combat, tempered and regulated by strict rules of proper competition. In a credit economy, planters, too, relied on personal trust and notes of hand for business transactions.

But, in the late eighteenth- and early nineteenth-century South, the commercial virtues of independence and reliability took on an intensely personal and emotional significance. They constituted a man's "honor"—and to question whether a man possessed such virtues involved physical risk. No family came to know those risks better than that of John Wright Stanly.

The honor of a gentleman was his reputation for independence, reliability, and physical courage. The gentleman could not be commanded or insulted by others. He was always in control of his own actions and could therefore be relied on for rigid personal honesty and for meeting every contractual obligation. His power to command him-

(Left). Dining room of the Stanly House. Courtesy Tryon Palace Restoration.

John Stanly (1774–1834). Portrait by an unknown artist, owned by John Gilliam Wood. N.C. State Archives.

Almost exactly coeval with the white John Stanly in New Bern lived a black John Stanly (1775–1833). Born a slave but emancipated in 1798, he built a fortune through his barbershops and plantations. A slaveowner himself, he freed twenty-three slaves between 1805 and 1818, including his wife and two children.

self as well as others set him apart completely from those who allegedly lacked these attributes most: poor whites, slaves, and women, who were known as "the weaker sex." In a system based on personal credit, honor had clear economic value and it also stood for the privileges of race, class, and sex. Vital to a gentleman's economic and social standing, it had to be defended at all costs. In a competitive society, others were always ready to advance their own positions by deliberately impugning the honor of their rivals. Insults were therefore not uncommon and the practice of dueling was the bloody result. A canny man, John Wright Stanly avoided the ultimate test of his reputation, but his heirs did not. Three of his five sons and at least one grandson participated in duels; two sons died and the other killed his opponent.

The survivor was John Stanly (1774–1833), the oldest of nine children and inheritor of his father's stately mansion. John Stanly idealized his father and seemed to justify his own imperious behavior by his father's example. "My father was as much superior to me as I am to common men," he is said to have arrogantly declared. All his life, he expected the obedience from others that a domineering father might have demanded from a submissive son. Trained as a lawyer and having no other source of income, John Stanly followed his father's example and launched his career by a judicious marriage. His bride was Elizabeth Franck, or Frank, whom one old New Bernian described as "a country heiress without cultivation, or opportunity . . . [who] inherited from her father, Martin Franck, large estates in Jones County which laid the foundations of Mr. Stanly's prosperity."

At an early age, the younger John Stanly threw himself into politics. He became Craven County's clerk and master in equity at the age of twenty-five, sat in the Seventh (1801–03) and Eleventh (1809–11) U.S. Congresses, represented New Bern for twelve terms in the lower house of North Carolina's General Assembly, and served two terms as its speaker. Contemporaries remembered him as a brilliant lawyer and a merciless debater. "In repartee and sarcasm I never saw his equal," one associate recalled. "His efforts in that line were absolutely withering. The composure of no suitor, witness, or rival advocate could survive his pungent criticism. Ever bold and fearless, he at once rose to the breadth of the occasion, always wielding a polished scimitar with the energy of a giant and the skill of an artist." It was artistry in sarcasm that led him to the dueling ground in 1803.

Stanly won election to Congress in 1801 over a fellow New Bernian and former North Carolina governor, Richard Dobbs Spaight. Republicans like Spaight were often just as aristocratic in private life as Federalists like Stanly, but they won popular approval by branding Federalism as undemocratic and injurious to rural interests. In 1802 Spaight sought election to the state Senate and Stanly worked against his election. By throwing doubt on Spaight's private adherence to

Richard Dobbs Spaight (1758–1802). N.C. State Archives.

Republican tenets, Stanly offended Spaight's honor as a gentleman and Spaight instantly called for "that satisfaction which one gentleman has a right to demand from another." Although at first Stanly averted the duel by a timely explanation, an escalating exchange of insults and insinuating handbills finally led to Stanly's challenge to Spaight, and a duel was set for 5:30 P.M. on 5 September 1802, in the rear of the Masonic hall on the outskirts of New Bern. The outraged gentlemen would not let any piddling city ordinance against gunfire stop them; the weapons were pistols at ten paces. An eager crowd of onlookers turned out to gawk at the spectacle.

The demands of honor were technically satisfied by a single exchange of shots, but, when the first pair of balls missed their targets, Spaight and Stanly kept firing. On the fourth round, Spaight fell wounded in the side and died the next day. Stanly was then twenty-eight years old. Spaight was fifty-four, roughly the age of Stanly's deceased father. The young man took refuge from prosecution in Virginia, but, confident that the law would not preclude a gentleman's right to defend his honor, he asked for executive pardon from Governor Benjamin Williams. The request was promptly granted, and Stanly continued his distinguished career without further interruption.

Gentlemen's use of violence to defend themselves against threatened domination by others spread down the social scale to combatants who could not be bothered with the punctilio of dueling. Fighting was common at market days, militia musters, elections, and other places where men gathered and liquor was freely available. William Attmore's visit to Washington, North Carolina, coincided with a militia muster. "Many disorders in town," the Philadelphian noted, "the militia some of them fighting. This is the practice every Muster-day." The same diarist noted brawls among celebrating legislators and hangers-on of the General Assembly, while Johann David Schöpf described a fistfight between two casual traveling companions.

Visitors were particularly horrified by the practice of "gouging." An antagonist in a brutal fight might twist his fingers in his opponent's hair to brace his hands, and then, "when these are fast clinched, the thumbs are extended each way to the nose, and the eyes *gently* turned out of their sockets." Drawing on numerous travelers' accounts, the Reverend Jedidiah Morse wrote in his *American Geography* (1789) that "the victor for his expertness, received shouts of applause from the sportive throng, while his poor, *eyeless* antagonist is laughed at for his misfortune." William Attmore witnessed the preliminaries of a fight in which gouging was proposed in a manner not dissimilar to a challenge to a duel in more polished circles. "They were going to fight out in the Road, when one of the company declared he wou'd massacre the Man who should attempt to Gouge. . . . Womble, one of the disputants declared 'I cannot fight without a Gouge.' One of the company supported his declaration saying 'Ay! A

Dueling pistols made in London in 1740 and used by Captain Hugh Waddell in the French and Indian War, in the Revolution, and in a duel in Southport, N.C. N.C. Museum of History Collection. N.C. State Archives.

Philadelphian Charles Biddle generalized about the men he met in North Carolina during the Revolution: "In point of talents he [Willie Jones] was one of the first men in America, but, like most Southern gentlemen, was too fond of horse racing and cards to attend much to business."

Gouge all weathers, by G—.'" Deterred perhaps by the prospect of blindness, the men called off their quarrel. "The terms were not accepted; their passions cooled by degrees and the gouging man said, 'tho I am but a little Shoemaker, I won't be imposed upon.'"

As an artisan, the shoemaker did not enjoy social or economic equality with gentry members like the Stanlys, and he may have been imposed upon by gentlemen every day, but he was powerless to resist his domination by the upper class. Threats of violence against his fellow artisans may have been Womble's way of compensating for his weak position in an unequal society, but the gouging shoemaker was scarcely alone. At every social level, North Carolina men squared off violently against each other in ritual declarations of personal independence.

Several commentators believed that fighting was an integral part of the culture of the slaveholding gentry. New England observers linked violence to gambling, drinking, and the whole gamut of non-puritanical pastimes. With stern disapproval, Jedidiah Morse reported that "the general topics of conversation among the men, when cards, the bottle, and occurrences of the day do not intervene, are negroes, the prices of indigo, rice, tobacco, &c." Asserting that Carolinians did not work as hard as New Englanders, Morse explained that "the citizens of North Carolina, who are not better employed, spend their time in drinking, or gaming at cards or dice, in cockfighting, or horse racing. Many of the intervals are filled up with a boxing match; and these matches frequently become memorable by feats of *gouging*." New England ministers were not alone in criticizing these activities. Apparently believing that the cause of American liberty demanded superior popular virtue and that there was something inappropriate about Carolina recreation, the Wilmington Committee of Safety endorsed the stricture of the First Continental Congress against "every species of extravagance and dissipation, especially all horse-racing, and all kinds of gaming, cockfighting, exhibitions of shows and plays and other expensive diversions and entertainments." The committee justified itself on the grounds that "nothing will so effectively tend to convince the British Parliament that we are in earnest in our opposition to their measures, as a voluntary relinquishment of *our favorite amusements*. . . . He only is the determined patriot who willingly sacrifices his pleasures on the altar of freedom [italics added]."

The pleasures condemned by Morse and the Wilmington committee did not really consume the energies of North Carolina citizens, and it would be unfair to suggest that idleness and dissipation were dominant features of North Carolina culture. Nevertheless, there were clear parallels between the work that North Carolinians did and the games they played. Fighting, whether between gentlemen at the dueling ground or between shoemakers in the inn yard, was part of the process of asserting one's privileges as a free white male. The copious consumption of liquor was another way for men to exhibit their personal prowess, whether in the grogshop, the drawing room, or the muster ground. Nonchalant gambling for high stakes displayed the size of a gentleman's estate and established his superiority to lesser mortals who had to worry about losing. Gambling at the race-track or the card table was thus an extension of the uncertain and competitive business activities that built the House in the Horseshoe and the John Wright Stanly House. The lavish balls, where dancing occurred, were further arenas for gentlemen and their ladies to display their finery and to size up each other's power. Like most people's games, North Carolinians' pastimes were very serious business.

These games grew out of the concerns of rural plantation society, but the reports we have of them originated from North Carolina's towns. In many ways, urban places provided the testing grounds and rewards of North Carolina's rural culture. The climax of commercial farming operations was not plowing, planting, or even harvest, but the sale of the crop in town. The perfect expression of rivalry among competing planters was not found in magnificent rural isolation, but in the lawsuit, the duel, or the contest for political office that frequently took place in an urban setting. The popular amusements that reflected the farmers' fundamental concerns were not only found among the joys of country life but also in the intermittent trips to town, where dancing, gambling, tippling, and the opportunity for display awaited the visiting families of gentlemen and yeomen alike. North Carolina towns were tiny, and their inhabitants were not typical of the state in the eighteenth century, but the state's urban settings satisfied deeply rooted needs of its overwhelmingly rural society. The urban vices deplored by President Joseph Caldwell were less eradicable than the well-meaning educator supposed.

William Attmore recorded North Carolinians' drinking habits: "It is very much the custom in North Carolina to drink Drams of some kind or other before Breakfast; sometimes Gin, Cherry-bounce, Egg Nog etc." On Christmas morning he wrote, "This Morning according to North Carolina custom we had before Breakfast, a drink of Egg Nog."

Hannah Johnston Iredell (1747–1826).
Portrait possibly by Jacob Marling. N.C.
State Archives.

The Culture of the Republic

In the early years of the 1770s, James Iredell of Edenton was young, indebted, and struggling. Repeatedly he wrote his parents and his benefactors, outlining for them his current problems and his steady and resourceful efforts to overcome them. Frequently he told his confidants of the goal that constantly lay before him. "I cannot expect every thing at once," he solemnly informed his mother in 1771, "[I] shall be only 20, Saturday, and all I wish for is enough to live upon independently." Addressing his patron and creditor, Henry Eustace McCulloh, the next year, Iredell vowed that "the sole object of my thoughts at present is how to extricate myself out of the Labyrinths I am in, and get into the [marvelous] Road that leads to Happiness and Independence." Months later, Iredell told his father that his prospects were looking up. "In England I must in any way be some years in a dependent and consequently an insecure position," he explained. "Here I have a tolerable certainty of something, tho' a mean one, and a probable expectation, by the fruits of my own Industry (all I depend upon with assurance) of procuring in the course of a few years a genteel Independency."

The independence that Iredell longed for was release from debt and from reliance on the patronage of others. He worked for the opportunity to take his place in the world of men as an autonomous gentleman, who lived well and relied on his own resources. Before he turned thirty, Iredell's hopes were fulfilled. His law practice was successful, he was an admired and trusted leader in North Carolina's government, and he was married to a wealthy and well-connected lady whom he loved very deeply. Of their four children, three would survive infancy and one, James Iredell, Jr., would become governor of the state and United States senator. As a man of affairs, a master, a husband, and a father, James Iredell had achieved his "genteel Independency."

His adopted state had done the same. "Independence" was a word that earlier generations of North Carolinians had shunned. When the Lords Proprietors held sway over the infant colony on the Albemarle, the inhabitants had acknowledged their constant need for help from Britain about as often as they protested the terms upon which that help was offered. "Wee need not Informe yor Lordshipps how weak & uncapable wee are of managinge things of so Concerne as y^e well layinge a foundation of a ^{C}ountry by wholsom Law wth out advertisement:& Direction from yor Lordshipp," read one humble and at least partially sincere petition of 1672. For a century there-

James Iredell (1751–99). Portrait by an unknown artist, owned by John Gilliam Wood. N.C. State Archives.

William Hooper (1742–90), son of a New England minister and one of three signers from North Carolina of the Declaration of Independence. N.C. State Archives.

after, the mother country remained a place that many colonists called "home," even though they had never seen it. Eventually, however, North Carolinians and other Americans became ready to strike out on their own. As early as 1761, Governor Arthur Dobbs had denounced "a republican spirit of Independency" in the pretensions of the colonial Assembly. Over the succeeding decade, Britain's efforts to tighten control over the colonies aroused furious resistance in North Carolina and the other colonies. By 1774 attorney William Hooper was predicting that all the colonies *are striding fast to independence, and ere long will build an empire on the ruin of Great Britain.*"

Two years later, the American Revolution had begun. The War for Independence grew out of a clash between the colonists' convictions about liberty and constitutional rights and the needs of the British Empire as determined by Parliament and the crown. Legalistic theories, however, were not the sole reason for the colonists' willingness to rebel. Free citizens fought for revolutionary ideas because the principles embodied key aspects of their daily social experiences. As James Iredell made clear, "independence" was a personal objective for North Carolinians just as it was a political objective for their state. Men as different from Iredell as John Allen, the pioneer Quaker who lived in a log cabin, and Philip Alston, the unruly planter who lived in a Piedmont mansion, shared Iredell's ambition to be free from coercive authorities. Their goals were shared by thousands of the Revolution's potential supporters throughout the colony. When illegal British taxes were first imposed by the Stamp Act, gentlemen and yeomen joined together readily under the slogan "Liberty, property, and no stamp duty," and their alliance continued until national independence had been won.

The colonists' fondness for liberty flourished in spite of the fact that inequality and a lack of freedom were widespread in their society. White men of the "middling" or "lesser sorts" found themselves restricted by the power and privileges of the "better sort" or gentry. Propertyless freemen had no legal right to vote. In the colonial assembly, an established elite of planters, merchants, lawyers, and other leading gentlemen from eastern towns and counties dominated the underrepresented farmers from the backcountry. Colonial women had virtually none of the rights that men had, and married women had no legal identities apart from their husbands. The gravest inequality and lack of liberty burdened the lives of the black slaves whose labor supported the privileges of white society. Colonial North Carolina was no egalitarian utopia.

From the beginning, some North Carolinians wanted to turn the traditionalist campaign for the rights of Englishmen to a more universal struggle for the rights of man. To a certain extent, they were successful. The new state constitution put strict limits on the power of government and gave the vote to propertyless male taxpayers. The Revolution itself tended to make men of talent leaders regardless of their social origins. In 1811 Jeremiah Battle of Edgecombe County recalled a Revolutionary hero who rose to the legislature on the basis of native ability. "Altho' he was almost destitute of education he was a considerable orator; & whenever he rose to speak in those public assemblies, the greatest attention was paid to his opinions, as they carried the strongest marks of good sense." In 1783 a Latin-American visitor, Don Francisco de Miranda, was likewise struck by the leveling effect of the Revolution on Carolina manners. Witnessing the celebration of American victory at New Bern, Miranda reported that "a barbecue (roast pig) was held at one o'clock, and a barrel of rum was opened. There was promiscuous eating and drinking, the principal officers and citizens mixing freely with the coarsest elements of society, all shaking hands and drinking out of the same glass."

Miranda's remarks were very illuminating. The Revolution had made civic equality the basic principle governing relations among white people, so the laborers, artisans, and tradesmen of New Bern had very good reasons to toast its outcome. But in spite of the ritual familiarity between the elite and the populace, Miranda made clear that the Revolution had hardly swept away class lines, even among white people. The new constitution limited the right to vote for state senators to the owners of fifty acres of land, and higher property requirements restricted access to elected offices. The rights of women and slaves were not improved by a fight for the liberty of white males, and the hierarchical principles of patriarchal and slave-based society continued. The legacy of the Revolution was therefore ambiguous. The outcome gave all citizens something to celebrate, but inequality and enslavement still persisted.

Landmarks of the War for Independence survive in every part of North Carolina, but the cultural monuments of independence, though less conspicuous than the battlefields, are even more significant. When the shooting died away, North Carolinians continued to work out the meaning of independence in the fabric of their daily lives and to fulfill the seemingly profound opportunities and obligations that liberty brought them.

As they shaped their new commonwealth, the citizens tried to follow the same principles that had led them initially to independence. The Provincial Congress made North Carolina a republic when it declared "that all political power is vested in, and derived from, the people only." Beginning as a political description, "republican" came to be a cultural standard that North Carolinians tried to apply to every institution in their society. When the citizens thought that their families, churches, schools, and economic arrangements were truly republican, they sought to protect that fragile quality from the hostile

Miranda's impression of American men was not flattering: "The men dress coarsely and carelessly. All smoke tobacco, usually in a pipe; and what is more, they chew it to great excess. Some have assured me that they could not rest or go to sleep without their chew in their mouth." Rippy, ed., "View of the Carolinas."

Penelope Barker organized the ladies of Edenton and five surrounding counties to support the American boycott of British imports, an effort known as the "Edenton tea party." The present Barker House postdates that event but is restored for visitors.

Moore's Creek National Military Park, Pender County, commemorates the battle site of a 1776 American victory over Tory Highland Scots.

Guilford Courthouse National Military Park, Guilford County, commemorates Lord Charles Cornwallis's Pyrrhic victory over the Americans under General Nathanael Greene in 1781.

83

Interior of Constitution-Burgess House, Halifax, Halifax County. This house was once thought to be the site of the drafting of the state's 1776 constitution, but a building no longer extant at the Eagle Hotel complex is now believed a likelier location. This house (ca. 1800) is restored as the town house and office of the lawyer Thomas Burgess.

forces of a changing world. If they thought their institutions failed to measure up to republican standards, the citizens sought appropriate reforms. The struggle to establish and maintain an independent republican society was the pervasive theme in North Carolina's history from 1770 to 1820.

Protecting the world of independent freeholders was the touchstone for North Carolina's republican doctrine. Institutions or public policies that tended to shore up that world were "republican"; those that undermined it were not. Predictably, not everyone agreed about the possible effects of various measures. Proponents of equality among white males insisted that the state be wary of entrenched privileges, concentrated private power, or the rise of aristocracy. More conservative republicans fought restrictions on the rights or the authority of the individual property holder, no matter how much land or how many slaves he had accumulated. Similarly, some republicans feared entanglement in the snares of the commercial economy, and cherished self-sufficiency as the secret to continued agrarian independence. The republican friends of economic development replied that no one could be independent who was poor and that the road to wealth led through the markets of the world economy. A debate over the nature of true republicanism therefore characterized North Carolina public life in the first generation of independence.

The stakes of the debate were high. For these North Carolinians, the future of liberty itself hung in the balance. "It will in great measure depend upon ourselves whether by our diligence and integrity we shall be a happy and respectable, or by our neglect or abuse of the great trust committed to us, a miserable and degenerate People."

More than three decades later, a sense of moral urgency still hovered over public life. Comparing America to God's chosen people, spokesmen warned incessantly that America's blessings were as fragile as those of the children of Israel. "We are indeed a favoured people," thundered Samuel Dickins, a congressional candidate in 1816. "It rests with ourselves whether we shall be so favoured for ages to come. . . . When we fall it shall be by the fatal effects of our own folly and vices." Armed with solemn moral purpose, and with a deep sense of how easy it would be to make a ruinous mistake, free North Carolinians took up the responsibilities of an independent society.

North Carolinians assumed their task with a seriousness that showed in the buildings they constructed as well as in the speeches they made. Architectural motifs from ancient Greece and Rome enjoyed a vogue as Americans tried to inculcate the sense of balance, moderation, and civic virtue thought to have been the hallmarks of those early republics. The Beaufort County Courthouse, though built many decades later, reflects these qualities. A triangular pediment of the roof directly over the entrance suggests the form of a Greek or Roman temple. A pair of delicately fan-shaped windows and an elaborately molded front doorway completed the decoration of this simple monument to republican government. Other early courthouses no longer extant featured comparable details. Similarly, the state's leaders designed the streets of Raleigh, the new capital, in a simple geometric form that reflected the practicality and directness of the new political order, but they also included five public squares as gathering places for an active and enlightened citizenry. The central square would contain the State House and would be called Union Square to indicate the importance of the federal government, and the four surrounding plazas would carry the names of notable North Carolina statesmen to commemorate the example of heroic local founding fathers.

Loyalists were a not insignificant proportion of North Carolina's population. Charles Biddle, a revolutionary and resident in the state for part of the war years, remembered the Loyalists: "I never felt the least angry with any of these people for their attachment to Great Britain; on political subjects every man has a right to enjoy his own opinion, and provided he does no mischief, should not be disturbed."

Beaufort County Courthouse (1819), Washington.

The most outstanding product of the cult of classical antiquity was the larger-than-life-size statue of George Washington that the legislature authorized in 1816. Completed by the great Italian sculptor Antonio Canova, the statue depicted the father of his country in the garb of a Roman general who has turned from the exercise of the sword to the arts of peace. Seated on a stool, the statesman was shown in the act of composing laws for the good of his countrymen. The figure of Washington touched a deep chord of emotion among North Carolinians; the *Raleigh Register* called it "that proud monument of national gratitude, which was our pride and glory," and most of its viewers seem to have agreed. As a work of political art, the sculpture was heavily didactic, and, according to a later legislative report, its message was plain. "While it refuted the calumny which stigmatizes republics as ungrateful," the solons declared, "it taught that true glory is the meed of virtue, and that, though temporary popularity may be gained by courting public favor, permanent renown, the renown which triumphs over the grave, is awarded to him alone who seeks the public good with pure and devoted disinterestedness." The citizens placed the image of Washington in the rotunda of the State House, where it silently demonstrated to legislators and visitors alike the glory of republican government and the qualities expected from an ideal republican statesman.

Public life was not the only arena in which North Carolinians explored the meaning of their newfound independence. Changes in personal life reflected a new sense of national self-confidence and the lure of new opportunities. Service in the Continental Army had given North Carolinians a chance to travel, to meet the inhabitants of other sections, and to prove their abilities under extraordinary conditions.

(Opposite) Canova's statue of Washington. N.C. State Archives. The statue lasted only briefly. A fire in 1831 destroyed the State House and reduced the masterpiece to blackened fragments. Efforts to restore it were unsuccessful, but in 1910 the Italian government gave North Carolina a plaster of paris copy of Canova's working model. In the 1960s a marble copy was made from the model and it now stands in the State Capitol (1834–40) as an eminent product of North Carolina's patriotic official culture.

As early as 1777 Ebenezer Hazard described Americans' reluctance to trust power in anyone's hands. Joseph Hewes, a signer of the Declaration of Independence for North Carolina, had not been returned to the Continental Congress, "as he has served 3 years, & the People think that a sufficient Length of Time for One Man to be entrusted with so much Power."

State Capitol (1794), which burned in 1831. Drawing by W. Goodacre. N.C. State Archives.

Daniel Boone. N.C. State Archives.

The Carson House (1780), Pleasant Gardens community, McDowell County, is built of foot-square logs covered with clapboard. It has beautiful hand-carved and paneled interior woodwork. The house served as an inn and stagecoach stop.

(Opposite) Zebulon B. Vance Birthplace (ca. 1795), Reems Creek Rd., Buncombe County.

Old methods of woodworking, cooking, spinning, weaving, and quilting are demonstrated during Pioneer Living Days at the Vance Birthplace.

Many "young men of the Revolution" seized the chance to get ahead in careers of public service and personal accomplishment. James Iredell perfected his legal abilities as attorney general of North Carolina and by 1790, at the age of 39, had become the youngest justice on the United States Supreme Court. John Wright Stanly built on his wartime business to become the state's largest importer and exporter.

For less prominent soldiers, the trans-Appalachian West beckoned as the country for a fresh start. North Carolina had promised western lands to Revolutionary War soldiers in lieu of more conventional payment. The Cherokees had been defeated along with the British, and the ministry's attempt to forbid settlement beyond the Blue Ridge perished with the other imperial policies; consequently the way was clear for large-scale white penetration of the North Carolina mountains. Following a trail blazed by North Carolina backwoodsman Daniel Boone, pioneers streamed across the ridges to the new states of Tennessee and Kentucky, or wound up rocky streams to the fertile coves tucked between the highest peaks of the mountain region.

David Vance was one of the settlers who chose the North Carolina side of the mountains. A veteran of the Continental Army and the Battle of King's Mountain, Vance came to the Reems Creek area of Buncombe County between 1785 and 1790 to work as a teacher, lawyer, and land surveyor. He purchased a farm from William Dever in 1795 that is now maintained as the birthplace of Zebulon Baird Vance, David Vance's grandson and the Civil War governor of North Carolina. The house on the property was built of logs, but it was larger and more elaborate than the typical settler's cabin, for David Vance was more prosperous than the average settler: he was a slaveholder who became first clerk of court for Buncombe County, colonel in the county militia, and representative in the General Assembly. The remote location of Colonel Vance's farm ensured that his family would continue to rely on traditional handicrafts to produce items for daily use in the home and on the farm. Once common in eastern and Piedmont North Carolina, these skills survived in the more recently settled mountains because the difficulty of access kept machine-made products at a distance until relatively later in the twentieth century.

Appalachia was not the only section of North Carolina to see new growth at the end of the eighteenth century. The Revolution had stripped Americans of the privileged terms of trade they had enjoyed in the British Empire: a postwar economic slump had been unavoidable. Two events of the early 1790s marked the end of these doldrums and gave North Carolinians and other Americans a renewed sense of economic opportunity. In 1792 a war broke out between revolutionary France and the great powers of Europe. The war lasted intermittently until 1815, and while Napoleon and his British adversaries kept the Old World torn by conflict, Americans reaped the

benefits by selling provisions and other raw materials to both sides. In 1793 a Connecticut tutor named Eli Whitney perfected a machine that could separate the seeds from the fibers of short staple cotton— a hardy upland plant that could thrive in the soil of most southeastern states. Whitney's gin removed the last technological bottleneck to full-scale mechanization of British textile manufacturing, and the Industrial Revolution was completely under way. Demand for the versatile fibers skyrocketed, and cotton cultivation spread across the American South from the coast to the Piedmont, and over the mountains into the fertile "Black Belt" soils of frontier Alabama and Mississippi. Conditions for cotton were ideal in the Deep South, but several North Carolina regions could produce the new crop too. The parallel rise of King Cotton and the Emperor Napoleon gave North Carolina republicans new access to prosperity and another reason to celebrate independence.

War and industrialization fanned demand for North Carolina staples like corn, pork, flour, and naval stores as well as cotton. The plantation economy thrived as large farms worked by slaves became the most efficient suppliers of North Carolina's popular exports. The old plantation regions of the east felt the new prosperity first but the planters' world also moved west as opportunities developed. Josiah Collins and the Reverend Charles Pettigrew grew rich on the shores

Eli Whitney's cotton gin.

One slave working a cotton gin could do what it had previously taken twelve slaves to do by hand. Before the invention of the gin, twenty-five slaves, working a hundred days, were needed to pick the seed from the cotton of one slave's produce for one growing season.

89

Latta Place (ca. 1800), Beattie's Ford Rd., north of Charlotte, Mecklenburg County, was built by a merchant-planter who, like Alexander, did his own peddling. Eventually prosperous, James Latta adorned his house with mirrors, gilt-framed pictures, and elaborate dressing cases from Philadelphia.

The Boston-born merchant and shipper William Rea kept a close eye on his business. "No one was permitted to remain idle about him. When his clerks were not otherwise engaged, he made them empty nail kegs and count nails, or rub hardware in the store, and the like." Winborne, *Colonial and State History*.

Rea's schooner *Belinda* and his brother's sloop *Phenix* brought to the Murfreesboro wharves West Indian rum, coffee, sugar, and molasses as well as limes, oranges, coconuts, and muslin.

of Lake Phelps by selling rice and corn to the combatants in Europe. Moore County's House in the Horseshoe witnessed the advantages of cotton culture during the residence there of Governor Benjamin Williams. In Mecklenburg County, immigrant peddler James Latta rode the cotton boom to planter status and left his mark on a substantial homestead known as Latta Place. To the north, Richard Bennehan made his sturdy farmhouse at Stagville in Orange County the center of a plantation domain that endured for five generations in the same family. In a foothills version of the same expansionary process, William Lenoir capped a successful career in land speculation by constructing an elegant mansion named Fort Defiance on the ruins of an obsolete outpost against the once-powerful Cherokees.

The expansion of commercial agriculture also stimulated the merchant's business, and new stores sprang up to market the planter's crops and supply him with the wares of distant places. William Rea's store in the new town of Murfreesboro is now the oldest commercial structure in North Carolina. Rea kept a retail shop on the first floor, while the heavy-duty hoist outside transferred bulky cotton bales and tobacco hogsheads to the upstairs warehouse. The same sort of business took place on a smaller scale at the tavern, store, and post office of Jethro Brown in Caswell County, where planters gathered to transact their business, enjoy a convivial glass, read the newspapers, and discuss the issues of the day in a neighborhood debating society that met there regularly around 1810. As they exercised their economic, cultural, and political freedoms, the new planters of Caswell County were shaping themselves and their peers into a self-confident and interconnected social class that would dominate North Carolina until the end of the Civil War.

Brown's Store (1804), Locust Hill, Caswell County. It is no longer a commercial building. N.C. State Archives.

90

The Bennehan House (ca. 1789–99), Stagville Plantation, Durham County, reflects the sturdy simplicity of this merchant-planter. Sited to catch the traffic, it was a way station for rich and poor alike who enjoyed the services of its store, blacksmith, and mill, or its hospitality.

In the established pattern of early surveyors, General William Lenoir speculated in land and accumulated wealth, which enabled him to build Fort Defiance (1789), N.C. #268 east of Patterson, Caldwell County, and furnish it handsomely. It was built by Thomas Fields according to a contract that specified a house forty by twenty-eight feet with four rooms on each of two floors and two staircases. Fields was paid in land. N.C. State Archives.

The William Rea Store (1790), Murfreesboro, Hertford County. Restored and adapted as a museum, the old store now displays among other exhibits a collection of agricultural implements.

Hope Plantation (1803), near Windsor, Bertie County.

Hope Plantation of Bertie County is a particularly striking example of North Carolina's expanding plantation society. Hope was the home of David Stone (1770–1818), U.S. senator and governor of North Carolina. He was the son of Zedekiah Stone, a Cashie River merchant and planter who had migrated from Massachusetts in 1766. A promising young man with good looks, impressive talents, and valuable connections, David Stone was graduated from Princeton with highest honors and read law under his fellow Princetonian William Richardson Davie of Halifax. Before Stone turned twenty, Bertie County freemen had sent him to the state convention that ratified the U.S. Constitution in 1789. They followed this honor with continuous terms in the North Carolina House of Commons until 1794, when David Stone won election to the bench as a superior court judge. Thereafter, Stone was never absent from public office until he left the U.S. Senate in 1814. Successively he was U.S. congressman, U.S. senator, judge again, governor of the state, member of the legislature, and once more U.S. senator. In spite of this long record of public confidence, Stone resigned from the Senate under fire, when his opposition to the War of 1812 stirred the anger of his North

Sampler by Governor David Stone's daughter. N.C. State Archives.

Drawing room at Hope Plantation.

Caretaker's residence, Hope Plantation, originally the Samuel Cox House (ca. 1800).

Carolina constituents. When he was only forty-eight in 1818, Stone died at Rest Dale, his plantation in Wake County.

Hope Plantation, however, was David Stone's original plantation and home. He received the land, 1,051 acres in all, as a wedding present from his father, one month before his marriage to Hannah Turner in 1793. In his farming operations, Stone's estate inventory shows that he continued some of the activities that had succeeded for his father. Like Zedekiah, David Stone raised corn and livestock and traded in lumber products, but instead of tobacco, rice, and naval stores he planted cotton. The change was evidently successful. When David Stone was serving his first term in the House of Commons, his father had owned 25 slaves and 1,078 acres of land. By the time Senator Stone died, he had accumulated some 138 slaves and 5,062 acres in Bertie County alone. Cotton clearly brought some North Carolinians a long way from the rustic life-style of the late colonial period.

The house that David Stone erected at Hope Plantation was the monument to his success. The newlywed husband began its construction on the basis of a plan he found in *The British Architect*, a builders' pattern book published by Abram Swann. The results were completed by 1803. Hope has two stories over an elevated basement. Chinese Chippendale balustrades ornament the double portico of the main entrance and the rooftop captain's walk. The two main rooms are on the second story. One was a long drawing room suitable for the balls and receptions so central to the gentry life-style. The other was a magnificent library with built-in shelves for the fourteen hundred volumes in David Stone's personal collection of books. The senator was both a gentleman and a scholar.

The excitement of independence spread through North Carolina's towns as well as through the countryside. Plantation products traveled through ports like New Bern on their way to American and foreign customers, and merchant communities battened on the growth of business. New Bern's population doubled between 1780 and 1800, and civic pride expanded correspondingly. Following their counterparts in other seaboard ports, New Bern's businessmen fostered a new style of building in their homes and public edifices as a proud expression of their autonomy and newly found prosperity.

The style has been called "Federal" in honor of the new United States, but it shared a great deal with the Georgian architecture that preceded it. Federal architecture was less massive than Georgian, the ornamentation was more delicate and more profuse, and the incorporation of Greek and Roman themes was more widespread and self-conscious. For a brief period, it became the most popular American style, and left its mark everywhere—from the porticos of the U.S. Capitol to the homes of North Carolina merchants.

The John Stevenson House is a good example of Federal domestic architecture in New Bern. It was built for a sea captain whose vessels plied the oceans between New Bern, New England, and the West Indies. The sea captain displayed his success with becoming republican simplicity. Like the typical Federal house in New Bern, the Stevenson House has a "side-hall" plan. A passage runs along the side of the house on all three floors, and two rooms open off each hall. Designed to save space, this plan is ideal for a town house where land is scarce. Also like other Federal houses, the interior woodwork is

The Stevenson House (ca. 1805), Tryon Palace Complex, New Bern, Craven County. Courtesy Tryon Palace Restoration.

Drawing of the New Bern Academy (1806), New Bern, from the Jonathan Price map, ca. 1819. N.C. State Archives.

especially fine in the Stevenson House. A wooden archway in the downstairs hall features a molding carved like a ship's cable. There are as many as twenty-four original Federal side-hall houses in New Bern today, each one differing from the others in the elaborateness of its details or in the quality of their execution, but all sharing the same basic features.

Three important public buildings remain from New Bern's Federal past: the Masonic Temple and Theater, the New Bern Academy building, and the First Presbyterian Church. As elsewhere in North Carolina, the Masonic order in New Bern was an exclusive fraternity of leading planters and townsmen who joined it to strengthen the personal, political, and economic ties that bound them together as an elite. When it was completed in 1809, the temple contained a theater and a ballroom for public entertainment and a meeting chamber for private ceremonies. Masonic ritual stressed mutual assistance, public service, and rational virtue; the classical lines of the temple and its mixture of public and private functions expressed the organization's principles directly. Like the Masonic Temple, the New Bern Academy catered to the gentry and also served a wider public. Chartered as a

In 1807, when George E. Badger attended the New Bern Academy his clothing included the following:

2 cambric cravats
3 pr cotton stockings
2 summer jackets
1 summer coat
4 summer waistcoats & 4 winter ditto
3 pr summer Panterloons & 3 pr ditto
7 linen shirts
1 winter jacket & 1 winter coat
4 Pocket Handkerchiefs

"Mr. Joseph Blyth has opened school in the public school-house. And will teach Latin, English, Arithmetic, Geography, Geometry, Trigonometry, and several other of the most useful branches of Mathematicks, according to the best and most approved methods. Gentlemen and ladies who favour him with their children may depend he will be diligent, and pay proper attention to their education." *North Carolina Gazette*, 24 July 1778.

private secondary school in 1764, the academy trained the sons of eastern North Carolina's leading families and a selected number of other students as well. One historian has declared that "this school had more influence upon the history of the state in the early years of the Commonwealth than any other save the University." Completed in 1806, the classical lines and elegant symmetry of the two-story brick schoolhouse were Georgian in basic plan and Federal in decorative details, much like the Masonic Temple. In function and appearance, both buildings encouraged an association between the leading classes of eastern North Carolina and the patrician citizens of the Roman Republic.

First Presbyterian Church, New Bern, Craven County, pictured before 1900. N.C. State Archives.

From an architectural standpoint, the outstanding Federal building in New Bern was the First Presbyterian Church, which was begun in 1819 and completed in 1822. Like New Bern's other impressive structures, the church is evidence of a dedicated body of civic leaders who wanted the best for themselves and for their small city and who possessed the means to obtain it. The church's finely carved woodwork and the balance of its proportions testify to a group of skilled craftsmen who could borrow designs from published sketches and shape them into a pleasing and original style. The popular motifs of Federal New Bern spread over eastern North Carolina, giving rise to a variety of graceful structures. The Sally-Billy House in Halifax is another good example of the region's unique Federal designs that expressed the values and prosperity of North Carolina's emerging republican leadership.

The self-assurance that stimulated architecture in New Bern and elsewhere and supported the expansion of diverse planters like David Stone, Benjamin Williams, James Latta, and Richard Bennehan rested on a growing commercial economy. National independence brought these men closer to the currents of international trade and gave them a personal status that rested on a complex interplay between agricultural production, the demand for staple crops, and world economic conditions.

The Sally-Billy House (1808), Halifax, Halifax County.

But what did liberty mean for the independent farmer who tilled the earth with his own hands, lived in a log cabin, and usually avoided stores and merchants as much as possible? According to Thomas Jefferson, these yeomen farmers and their families were the ideal citizens of a republic. "Those who labor in the earth," Jefferson wrote, "are the chosen people of God, if ever he had a chosen people, whose breasts he has made his peculiar deposit for substantial and genuine virtue." For Jefferson and for his North Carolina neighbors as well, public virtue and not wealth or aesthetic expression was the supreme test of a republic. Did pedimented porticos and Chinese Chippendale balustrades have anything to do with the great body of the American people or with the moral conditions of their republic?

As the eighteenth century drew to a close, many North Carolinians were deciding that the dominant culture of the republic was unsatisfactory to them. For one thing, the cultural world that embraced Federal architecture, Masonic ritual, and the cult of classical antiquity was the private preserve of an exclusive elite. Common freemen in North Carolina were closed off from the education, leisure, and powerful social positions that made this culture meaningful to the gentry, and they were often made to feel inferior because they did not share in the gentry's "refinement." These citizens also lacked the economic advantages provided by the expansion of the market economy. Numerous quiet citizens found a public life dominated by fighting, gambling, and drunken electioneering morally repugnant.

The Reverend George Micklejohn (ca. 1717–1817), who remained in America after the Revolution, shocked his more orthodox colleagues by his outspoken Deism. Henry Pattillo wrote to Charles Pettigrew in 1788: "Our Episcopalians are getting Mr. Micklejohn to N[ut] B[ush] in the month. I heard him last visit. He is an artist at avoiding Jesus Christ, both in nature and substance. The first thorough deistical sermon I ever heard." Lemmon, *Pettigrew Papers*.

John Norwood's letter to William Lenoir, 20 April 1798, tells a similar story: "I never understood Deism was preached till lately, a person . . . said to be a man of education, preached in favour of it some time past, at Halifax, Warrenton, and Wmsborough in Granville, his discourses were highly approv'd by most of the Rich, the fashionable and polite, and his performances by them, profusely Rewarded."

Thomas Coke, an English clergyman associated with Wesley, described Edenton in 1785: "I went to Edenton, a most wicked place. Here Mr. Pettigrew preaches. The people in general seemed to prefer the courthouse, which is an elegant place, so I went there accordingly, and preached to a large congregation. . . . There seemed nothing but dissipation and wickedness in the tavern at which I put up, and yet the landlord would take nothing for my dinner. . . . I suppose Mr. Pettigrew does as much good in Edenton as a little chicken." Grissom, *History of Methodism*.

They had reason to be disappointed that the Revolution had failed to complete its promises of liberty, equality, and progress for everyone.

There were also signs of a spiritual and moral crisis in North Carolina and the rest of the nation. Although the eighteenth-century gentry admired what they regarded as enlightened and rational virtue, they often had minimal faith in divine revelation. A philosophy called "Deism" grew popular. It held that God had originally created the universe but had left it alone to operate by scientific laws ever since. Writing to a friend in 1797, Joseph Caldwell, a young instructor at the University of North Carolina, summed up the situation frankly. "In North Carolina and particularly in the part east of Chapel Hill everyone believes that the way of rising to respectability is to disavow as often, and as publicly as possible the leading doctrines of the Scriptures. They are bug-bears, very well fitted to scare the ignorant and weak into obedience to the law; but the laws of morality and honor are sufficient to regulate the conduct of men of letters and cultivated reasons." For wealthy and educated Deists, unaided human reason was enough to guarantee the moral success of the republic, but more pious North Carolinians felt the need of religious guidance too.

The churches of colonial North Carolina had frequently been the national churches of pioneer immigrant groups. The Church of England itself was the most obvious example, and the colonial government had provided it with legal privileges and public subsidies.

St. John's Episcopal Church (1773), Williamsboro, Vance County, the oldest surviving frame church in the state.

Interior, St. John's Episcopal Church.

The colony built several beautiful Anglican Churches at public expense in eastern towns and counties, but could not make the Church of England a spiritual home for the common people. Nutbush Church, now known as St. John's Church in Williamsboro, was a balanced and harmonious architectural gem. It was constructed in 1773 by John Lynch, a master carpenter. Tobacco planters flocked to its services from all corners of Granville County, but sincere dissenters objected that the ministers there preached Deism and they would not tender it their support. Other localities complained that the missionary priests sent out from England were immoral and incompetent drunkards. All the Anglican churches in North Carolina fell into disuse after the Revolution cut off their subsidies and supply of ministers. Even when Anglicans reorganized themselves as the Protestant Episcopal church, they made little headway with the populace.

Zion Lutheran Church, Mt. Pleasant Rd., four miles south of Faith, Rowan County. It was popularly known as "Organ Church" after 1774, when John Stirewalt built an organ for it. The present structure dates from 1795 except for a higher roof and a steeple.

St. Paul's Lutheran Church (1808), west of Newton, Catawba County, was built by a carpenter named Henry Cline. He gave it the finest early nineteenth-century ecclesiastical interior in the Piedmont.

The churches of the other immigrants were in a different situation. The Germans had strong religious roots in their Piedmont settlements and their traditions continued after the Revolution as before. The Moravians constructed Bethabara Church in 1788, and Lutherans and German Reformed worshipers built comparable structures like Zion Church in Rowan County and St. Paul's Church in Catawba County. Ethnically based Presbyterian churches were also active among the Scotch-Irish and the Scottish Highlanders, but, like the Germans, many of these congregations worshiped in a foreign language. Except for some Scotch-Irish clergy, their ministers had limited appeal beyond their particular nationalities. The colonial churches of North Carolina could not match the spiritual aspirations of many thousands of post-Revolutionary state citizens.

100

Passed over by the economic and political order, isolated from the gentry's republican culture, scandalized by Deism, and unsatisfied by traditional churches, thousands of nonelite Carolinians turned to dissenting Protestant ministers who came from the same social backgrounds as themselves. Joseph Caldwell described these preachers condescendingly. "One reason why religion is as scouted from the most influential part of society," he explained, "is that it is taught only by ranters, with whom it seems to consist only in the powers of their throats and the wildness and madness of their gesticulations and distortions." The fervor of evangelical preaching was indeed unconventional to those more used to academic-style sermons, but most itinerant preachers had little interest in trimming their pulpit styles to suit more sedate tastes.

Radical Protestants often had a low opinion of upper-class culture, regarding it as frivolous and worldly at best, unjust and wicked at worst. In extreme cases, religious social criticisms touched on slavery itself, the institution that laid the foundation of the planters' power over others. North Carolina Quakers began to criticize slavery and to free their slaves in the eighteenth century, but resentment of bondage and the power it gave to the gentry did not stop with the Society of Friends. In an angry letter to the Reverend Charles Pettigrew, the Episcopal planter-priest of Tyrrell and Washington counties, local Baptist spokesman Amariah Biggs had trouble with his spelling, but he made his message clear. "Sir," he began, "I Labour trewly and honestly to get my one Living In that State of Life which It has pleased god to Call me and am Contented theirwith but you are not so[.] you put the yoke of Iron on the poor Ethiopens and get your riches by their rod of oppression[.]" Evaluating Pettigrew's economic, political, and religious role in the county, Biggs drew a literally damning conclusion. "The Scripture saith tis Easir for a Camel to go through the Eye of an needel then for a rich man to Enter into the Kingdom of heaven[.] I have greater reason to believe that at the last day . . . You will be found at the Left of the throne of the magesty on high Where you will call for a drop of water to Cool your tungue seeing that all ready tis on fiers of hell." Not all evangelicals were so positive about the gentry's future prospects. More commonly, the dissenting ministers merely shrugged off the planters' culture, unless it could be rededicated to religious purposes. Thus Methodist pioneer Francis Asbury noted in his journal that the town of New Bern contained a "famous house, said to be designed for the masonic and theatrical gentlemen," and then noted dryly, "it might make a most excellent church." Armed with faith that gave them the necessary confidence to distance themselves from the gentlemen of New Bern, Asbury and his colleagues launched a religious movement that came to dominate North Carolina's popular culture in the century to come.

The crusade was known as the Great Revival. It embraced a

Lower Stone Church, the popular name for Grace Church, founded near Rockwell, Rowan County, by German settlers. It was begun in 1795 and finished in 1811. The original stone floor and goblet-shaped pulpit have been replaced and a belfry added.

"I came to the Dutch Church & heard two Sermons in their own Tongue & one in English," William Ormond recorded in his diary, 19 July 1802.

Aptly called the "Prophet of the Long Road" by Ezra Tipple, Asbury spent almost forty-five years, averaging six thousand miles a year, traveling and preaching, often in great physical discomfort and illness. In 1783 he wrote: "hitherto the Lord has helped me through continual fatigue and rough roads; little rest for man or horse, but souls are perishing—time is flying—and eternity comes nearer every hour."

Exposed to the rigors of travel and makeshift shelter, any itinerant preacher could have duplicated William Ormond's accommodations one night in 1792: "At bed time three of the Children & myself lodged in an indifferent bed in an open house, & the Man & Woman lay on the dirt floor before the fire."

Caldwell's log college, in Guilford County, was supposed to have been modeled on a similar school Caldwell knew in his native Pennsylvania: a two-story structure of squared-off logs and central chimney.

The black freeman and preacher Henry Evans exerted such a good influence on the morals of his slave adherents that their masters welcomed his preaching in Fayetteville, supported his efforts, and attended his services.

"In the latter part of that year [1775] . . . we had the greatest revival of religion, I have ever seen. I have been at meetings where the whole congregation would be bathed in tears: and sometimes their cries would be so loud that the preacher's voice could not be heard. Some would be seized with a trembling, and in a few moments drop on the floor as if they were dead; while others were embracing each other, with streaming eyes, and all were lost in wonder, love, and praise." *Memoir of the Reverend Jesse Lee.*

variety of churches, individuals, and groups, but the most important denominations involved were the Baptists, Methodists, and Presbyterians. The movement's hallmark was evangelicalism, or an emphasis on personal conversion as the test of Christian salvation. Without an overwhelming personal experience of rebirth, evangelicals held that no amount of good deeds or pious thoughts could justify a person in the sight of God. To the humble individual, the evangelical churches offered a reassurance and a source of personal esteem that did not depend on riches, status, or education. To the collective body of believers, the churches offered a vision of the virtuous republic that did not depend on classical erudition, European nationality, or invidious class distinctions.

The evangelical denominations grew steadily throughout the latter half of the eighteenth century. Methodist Bishop Francis Asbury and dozens of local circuit riders crossed and recrossed North Carolina, preaching at farms, inns, and crossroads whenever anyone would listen. Baptists received an important boost from the arrival of the Reverend Shubal Stearns from Connecticut, and the rapid emergence of the six churches of the Sandy Creek Baptist Association that soon followed him. The Reverend David Caldwell's "log college" in Guilford County prepared dozens of young men for the Presbyterian ministry and exposed them to the fiery eloquence of northern-trained evangelists. Log churches appeared in numerous communities, offering an institutional home for new converts after the traveling preachers had moved on.

The evangelicals directed their message to all who felt demeaned or disfranchised by the "World," or in this case, by North Carolina's dominant hierarchical culture. Those who responded were frequently young people, white yeomen and artisans, women of all classes, and slaves. Blacks were not treated the same as whites in the churches, but the evangelical denominations came closer than any other white institutions to recognizing the spiritual equality of all men and women. Some masters opposed slave conversions for exactly this reason, but others encouraged it, supposing that religion would make the slaves more contented with their lot. Slaves seem to have embraced the new religion because it gave them an opportunity to acknowledge the obvious power of Western culture while condemning the sin of their own enslavement. The mass conversion of Afro-Americans from traditional African religions probably dates from this period, although the process undoubtedly continued for many decades. Like the slaves, ordinary white North Carolinians joined the churches at least in part because they wished to reject the cultural values of those who stood above them in the eyes of the "World."

The piecemeal process of conversion reached explosive proportions in the Great Revival of 1801–5. Beginning in the summer of 1801, word trickled back to Orange and what is now Alamance

County of remarkable works of God in the frontier state of Kentucky. Several ministers had moved west from these Piedmont communities, and thousands had gathered to hear their preaching at a place called Cane Creek. Assembled in huge crowds, multitudes of convicted sinners had cried out, wept, and fainted in near despair. When the possibility of salvation began to glimmer hopefully before them, the new converts manifested their joy with extraordinary physical "exercises." They laughed, sang, trembled, jerked uncontrollably, and even barked like animals. Many doubted that such undignified behavior could truly come from God, but others were convinced that the revival was a genuine visitation of the Holy Spirit. In October 1801 the friends of revival held the first five-day camp meeting in North Carolina at Hawfields Presbyterian Church, in Orange (now Alamance) County. They hoped for a repetition of the Kentucky phenomenon and they were not disappointed. Camp meetings spread through the state and soon the entire upper South was ablaze with the spirit of revival.

Inevitably, enthusiasm eventually waned and opposition roused itself. The Reverend Charles Pettigrew complained that his parishioners "were warmed, but not instructed" by the revival. "Their religion was placed in their passions, & these are now cooled, & their religion is fled. . . . Their last State is worse than the first," Pettigrew concluded sadly. Not unmindful of this possibility, evangelicals sought to counter it with institutions that would capture and preserve the intense emotions that the revival had evoked. They built new churches first of all, and later they would turn to Sunday schools, prayer meetings, temperance societies, denominational colleges, and annually scheduled camp meetings.

The Mount Pleasant Methodist Church in Forsyth County was among the new congregations formed in the wake of the Great Revival. Located on a hill overlooking the Yadkin River and now on the grounds of Tanglewood Park, Mount Pleasant bears the date 1809 on one of its timbers. Moravian documents from nearby Salem record that camp meetings were held there regularly as early as 1810. More prosperous than most early Methodist congregations, the members of Mount Pleasant church were able to house their meeting in a frame building instead of a log cabin. Inside, a gallery seated slaves, who formed a part of every early Methodist congregation. Downstairs, the room is severely plain. No cushions pad its high-backed pine benches; no carpet covers its bare wooden floor. The worshipers came to praise God and to hear the preached word. They would not be distracted by worldly decoration.

One effect of churches like Mount Pleasant was to rekindle seriousness of purpose in rural North Carolina society. The evangelicals took their converts into a disciplined new world where no vain pastimes or frivolous amusements were permitted to distract the

Cross Roads Presbyterian Church (1779), N.C. #119 north of Mebane. Alamance County, was the site where North Carolina's Great Revival began at a communion service in August 1801.

John A. Cameron wrote to his brother Duncan on 12 October 1808 about a camp meeting: "As I passed through Montgomery I passed by a great Camp Meeting—there were many hundreds collected. A Mr. McIntyre preached in the Gaelic and a Mr. McMillan in the English language; being quite a novelty to me, I stopped, tied my horse and walked into one of the congregations. The greatest decorum presided, the preachers were zealous in the cause and the audience attentive. There was a vast number of Scots from Moore there."

Mount Pleasant Methodist Church (1809), Tanglewood Park, Forsyth County, was built by Henry Eccles. He left his initials and the building date in a central support.

Interior, Mount Pleasant Methodist Church.

believer from his godly mission or to disturb the solemnity of his sanctified life. Drinking, gambling, dancing, cardplaying, theater-going, and Sabbath-breaking were strictly forbidden, and violators faced suspension or expulsion from church if they did not mend their ways and repent. Not by coincidence, these were the vices of the planter aristocracy, who frequently placed the evangelicals beneath themselves in social dignity.

Writing in 1810 and 1811, scattered observers of North Carolina were unanimous that the revival had a pervasive influence on popular mores. A correspondent from Moore County reported to a Raleigh newspaper that "formerly cock-fighting, Gander-pulling, Horse Racing, and card playing, were the principal Amusements—The present religous impressions of the people has laid aside the two former as cruel and barbarous and contrary to benevolence and humanity." He also believed that gambling and fox hunting were likewise on the decline. From Edgecombe County, Jeremiah Battle observed that gambling was declining but that dancing and family visiting had become the favorite amusements. A Duplin County writer mentioned cards, racing, and dancing, "but these Amusements are now much Neglected where religion Progresses." Having fun did not become extinct in North Carolina, but it certainly became less boisterous and less conspicuous. In place of idle amusements, the churches gave their members a new experience, a new community, and a new measure of themselves as human beings.

The initial impact of churches like Mount Pleasant was strongest among the middle and lower classes of rural society, but the appeal of the evangelical churches eventually spread up the social scale. Hardworking middle-class Christians began to get ahead in life, and pious wives of planters converted their husbands and children. Perhaps most importantly, evangelicals decided it was more important to convert slaves than to criticize slaveholders. They exchanged the vision of a morally perfect society in this world for the goal of a converted society fully prepared for the world to come. Planters came to see the advantages of a sober, united, church-going population. As Caswell County planter Bartlett Yancey noted in 1810, "the great revival of religion . . . seems to have contributed much to the dissemination of morality, sound principles and good order in society." Acting on Yancey's insight, planters began to give the evangelical movement their support and even opened themselves to hear its message.

By 1819 religion had gained great prestige among the gentry, according to the grandson of a North Carolina signer of the Declaration of Independence. In a sermon of that year preached to the well-heeled founders of the North Carolina Bible Society, the Reverend William Hooper recalled the days "when religion with downcast eye and timid step never ventured to approach the mansions of the opulent and polite, and only found casual entertainment among the cottages of the poor and ignorant." Hooper rejoiced with his audience that the churches "had grown respectable in the eyes of men" and had won the allegiance of "the men occupying the station and possessing the political influence of those who are now the patrons and pillars of our Bible Society." As North Carolina's commitment to evangelical religion deepened, the churches' style and doctrine became fixed features of the people's common culture. Beginning as a spiritual challenge to the established order, the churches became a part of it, and gave their blessing to North Carolina's stable, agrarian, and republican way of life.

The most conspicuous collaborative project of the planters and the evangelicals was the University of North Carolina. Led by General William Richardson Davie, prominent secular politicians believed that a university to train each rising generation of the elite in the principles of science, reason, and virtue would be an incomparable asset for the future of North Carolina. Prominent Presbyterian clergy, inspired by the Reverend Samuel E. McCorkle, hoped that a religiously oriented school would train future ministers in Greek, Latin, and moral philosophy, while preparing other godly youths for honorable service in other fields. Both groups urged the legislature to act, and the University of North Carolina was the result.

Chartered in 1789, the college opened in 1795 as the first state university in America. McCorkle wrote the first curriculum; it stressed moral education and the classical languages of Latin and New Testament Greek. A little later, the trustees substituted a different course of study proposed by Davie. The new curriculum was more practical, stressing modern languages and mathematics. If his parents chose, the student could avoid the "dead" languages altogether and earn an English diploma that was based on the study of science, mathematics, and their practical applications. In Davie's view, there was more virtue to be found in useful skills for the new country than in the ambiguous speculations of philosophers, theologians, and dead poets. Under the Reverend Joseph Caldwell, the university's second president, a compromise was struck that provided for more secular versions of the traditional classical subjects.

When it opened, the university met in a new building that foreshadowed Davie's curriculum far more than McCorkle's. Severely practical, the structure now known as Old East was a barn-like pile of plain brick that housed the students, tutors, and classrooms. Only an ordinary band of decoration at the roofline accented the triangular pediments and suggested the appearance of a classical temple. The University of North Carolina would sponsor no more than a rough-hewn enlightenment.

A simple but forceful lesson in the social and economic differences between North Carolina and the neighboring state of Virginia comes from a glance at their respective state universities. After he

General William Richardson Davie (1756–1820). N.C. State Archives.

University of North Carolina 1797.

Sketch of the state university's first building, Old East, Chapel Hill, Orange County, as it originally looked to John Pettigrew, a student in 1797. Begun in 1793, it was to cost five thousand dollars and to contain sixteen rooms and four passages.

In June 1796 one of the first students to have enrolled described conditions at Chapel Hill in a letter to John Haywood: "The University and every thing about it are much as they were when you left them. Improvements of no kind have been made. The number of students has increased to ninety four, and room for more cannot possibly be had here—I have read through Geography, the English Grammar and have cifered through Arithmetic on which I expect to be examined in July, that I understand them I will not promise you—

"The provision furnished by the Steward consists chiefly of Bacon, Beef & Mutton; no luxurious Diet, but strong wholsome Food very fit for laborious Men, but by no means suited to the Organs of Sensation—" Ernest Haywood Papers.

left the White House in 1809, Thomas Jefferson designed an "academical village" at the University of Virginia that would rank as a triumph of American Greek Revival architecture. No such extravagance tempted North Carolina. Though the state had fostered a modest plantation economy, great wealth and superlative cultural achievements still eluded her citizens. North Carolina planters' sons would study their lessons in the simplest possible quarters, while the scions of the Old Dominion's aristocracy would learn to love the classics in exquisite surroundings, each one in his own miniature Monticello.

The obvious contrast between Old East in Chapel Hill and the Rotunda at Charlottesville was seen by later North Carolinians as a sign of North Carolina's inferiority relative to the rest of the Union. Though foreign war and the cotton boom had stimulated the state's economy, other states had profited too, and most had done better than North Carolina. The tide of immigration that had flooded the Carolina backcountry in the middle of the eighteenth century had veered across the mountains after the Revolution, and North Carolina's relative rank in population dropped from third in 1790 to fifth in 1830. Persistent geographical obstacles barred her citizens from the highest profits of the new commerce, and many state citizens began to contemplate removal to the richer cotton lands of the Southwest. In spite of the significant gains that had appeared since the Revolu-

106

tion, the changes were not enough for North Carolina to keep up. By 1815 the state had come to seem backward.

More than local pride was at stake in the question of North Carolina's development. The emigration movement damaged land values for those who left and those who chose to stay. Departing planters took large numbers of slaves with them, and land and slaves were the principal components of the state's meager tax base. Declining population spelled frustration and political impotence for North Carolinians ambitious for preferment in the U.S. Congress, the courts, or the executive branch. Migration drove families apart, and forced energetic youths to choose between their parents and their futures. Most fundamentally, perhaps, economic decline reflected poorly on the republican experiment, and reminded a younger generation that they had not lived up to the towering achievements of their illustrious founding fathers. As the 1820s approached, North Carolinians were facing a painful dilemma, for the dream of independence was in danger of being lost.

The question was what to do about it. A substantial and respectable body of opinion maintained that the wisest course was to do nothing. Led by Senator Nathaniel Macon, conservatives warned that backwardness was not the only danger that North Carolinians

University of Virginia. Engraving by B. Tanner. Courtesy University of Virginia.

107

Buck Springs Plantation House (1783), four miles north of Vaughan on S.R. #1345, Warren County, before it was burned but not completely destroyed in 1976. Nathaniel Macon, a powerful and influential Congressman for thirty-seven years, built this modest frame house of one room, sixteen feet square, with a cellar and a loft. Though charred and roofless it still stands along with a smoke house. The family graves are near the restored corn crib.

faced. The kind of greatness desired by the reformers would carry North Carolina further and further from the world of self-sufficiency to the networks of international trade. No matter how backward he seemed, the independent freeholder owed nothing to anybody. The bustling entrepreneur depended on a hundred different parties for one essential item or another, and failure on their parts could drag him into ruin. The independent republic could best preserve itself by keeping such operators at a distance.

Macon and his associates went one step further. Observing the pace of social and economic development in other portions of the Union, they noticed that rapid change led men to think that anything was humanly possible. Macon scoffed at the miracles of steam technology and at what he called "the fashionable & favorite expression,

The massive corn crib on Macon's Buck Springs Plantation, S.R. #1345, four miles north of Vaughan, Warren County. Photograph by Randall Page. N.C. State Archives.

"Don't live near enough to your neighbor to hear his dog bark" was Nathaniel Macon's advice. Quoted by Jonathan Daniels, "North Carolina," *Holiday*, October 1947.

'to conquer Space'" and at the notion that "the power of science was omnipotent, it could do everything." What if the quest for a perfect society should lead men to question the institution of slavery? Looking at the emerging moral reform movements of the North, Macon did not like what he saw. Reformers had brought about abolition of slavery in the states beyond the Mason-Dixon line, and the lesson for white North Carolinians was clear: progress of all kinds was dangerous. "Why depart from the good old way" Macon pleaded from the floor of the U.S. Senate. "[It] has kept us in quiet, peace, and harmony—every one living under his own vine and fig tree, and none to make him afraid. Why leave the road of experience, which has satisfied all, and made all happy, to take this new way, of which we have no experience. The way leads to universal emancipation." For Macon, independence for white people required that black people remain slaves, and, in order to preserve white supremacy, he was perfectly willing to stop all sorts of progress in its tracks.

Some North Carolina politicians thought Nathaniel Macon was unnecessarily alarmist. They were confident that republican government was equal to any task the people gave it. How could anyone be independent who was poor, they inquired, and how could North Carolina prosper when private initiative alone lacked the power or the

The North Carolina State Bank (1818), New Bern Ave., Raleigh, Wake County, now houses the State Credit Union. Photograph by Tony Vaughn. N.C. State Archives. It was built with a vault, offices, and housing for an employee, but altered in 1873 for use as the rectory of Christ Church.

Remains of the Roanoke Canal's Chockoyotte Aqueduct, near Weldon, Halifax County. Photograph by Catherine Bishir. N.C. State Archives. The construction (ca. 1819–23) was an engineering feat of its time.

incentive to restructure the state's economy? Governor William Miller was as much a supporter of independent farmers as Nathaniel Macon was, but he wished to protect them a different way. Repeating republican clichés in his 1816 address to the legislature, Miller praised agrarian life as "the parent of health, plenty, and contentment; the nurse of patriotism and every virtue." However, he added, "agriculture . . . flourishes most where she can, with ease, pour her superabundant stores into the lap of a liberal market. Thus situated, commerce, the mechanic arts, and their fruits, the comforts and elegancies of life, follow in her train." North Carolina should foster economic development by undertaking the "improvement of our roads, cutting canals, and opening the navigation of our rivers," or, in other words, by sponsoring what the nineteenth century called "internal improvements."

The outstanding reformer Archibald D. Murphey had a similar message for the 1815 General Assembly. "The time has come," intoned the senator from Orange County, "when it behooves the legislature of North Carolina to provide efficiently for the improvement of the inland navigation of the state. To delay this provision is to postpone that national wealth, respectability, and importance which only follow in the train of great internal improvements." When transportation costs were made lower by the construction of canals, Murphey argued, prosperity would ensue, and North Carolina could take its rightful place in the world of progressive republican independence.

The visions of Nathaniel Macon and Archibald Murphey were radically different, but both were logical versions of North Carolina's republican ideals. Both stressed the independence of the individual white freeholder and promised to guard his world from external assault and internal corruption. Macon sought to protect the institution of slavery by sealing off the influence of destabilizing social change. Equally devoted to slaveholders' interests, Murphey sought to strengthen the plantation economy by cutting the planter's freight rates and by enabling the isolated yeoman to sell the crops and buy the slaves that would raise him to planter status too. Each in his own way, Macon and Murphey were legitimate heirs of North Carolina's eighteenth-century republican heritage.

Achibald DeBow Murphey (1777–1832). N.C. State Archives.

Development was uneven, but the path that North Carolina chose was closer to Murphey's than to Macon's. Before the Orange County senator ever filed his famous reports calling for reform, the legislature had chartered the State Bank of North Carolina to provide the credit that would ease the transition to an intensified market economy. The bank's original building stands as a handsome Federal monument to the ideals of republican commerce. As Macon was uttering his direst warnings, the state was chartering navigation companies to speed the shipment of staples along North Carolina's shallow rivers. Perhaps the most successful corporation was the Roanoke Navigation Company, which opened the water route for cotton and tobacco to float down the Roanoke River to Albemarle Sound. The centerpiece of the company's improvements was a short canal around the river's waterfalls at Weldon. The stone locks of this canal are still in place, and the aqueduct that carried the waterway over Chockoyotte Creek on the outskirts of Weldon is an outstanding example of the engineer's genius and the stonemason's skill.

Banks and internal improvements did not remake North Carolina overnight, but the cumulative changes they introduced did reorient the economy of the state to the demands of national and international commerce. They also strengthened the grip of the slave plantation on the life of the state, committed North Carolina politicians to the inflexible defense of slavery itself, and set the stage for a bloody sectional conflict. The social and economic revolution wrought by internal improvements in the nation at large were more profound than any material outcome of the War for Independence itself.

These changes were hardly visible in 1820. The nostalgic world of Nathaniel Macon still looked viable from his simple cottage at Buck Spring plantation in Warren County. The debate he fought with the advocates of development still raged for a generation or more longer. The mere existence of the controversy was nevertheless a measure of how much the lives of North Carolinians had changed within the framework of their independent society.

Interior of the Burgwin-Wright House
kitchen (1771), with an unusual split-
step ladder to the upper floor. Lord
Cornwallis used the Burgwin-Wright
House as his headquarters when the
British occupied Wilmington.

Bibliography

Printed Sources

Allen, Beulah Oyama, comp. *Allen House and Some of its Allens.* Nashville, 1980.

Anderson, Jean B. "A Preliminary Report on Stagville Plantation: The Land and the People." Report, N.C. Division of Archives and History, 1977.

Asbury, Francis. *Francis Asbury in North Carolina: The North Carolina Portions of The Journal of Francis Asbury.* Edited by Grady L. Carroll. Nashville, 1964.

Ashe, Samuel A. *A Biographical History of North Carolina, from Colonial Times to the Present.* 8 vols. Greensboro, 1905–17.

Attmore, William. "Journal of a Tour to North Carolina." In *James Sprunt Historical Publications,* vol. 17, no. 2. Chapel Hill, 1920.

Bartram, William. *The Travels of William Bartram.* Edited by Mark Van Doren. New York, 1940.

Bassett, John Spencer. *Slavery in the State of North Carolina.* Baltimore, 1899.

Battle, Kemp Plummer. *History of the University of North Carolina: From Its Beginning to the Death of President Swain, 1789–1868.* Vol. 1. Raleigh, 1907.

———. "Letters of Nathaniel Macon, John Steele, and William Barry Grove." In *James Sprunt Historical Publications,* vol. 3. Chapel Hill, 1902.

Bernard, John. *Retrospections of America, 1797–1811.* New York, 1887.

Bernheim, G. D. *History of the German Settlements and of the Lutheran Church in North and South Carolina.* Philadelphia, 1872.

Bernheim, G. D., and Cox, George H. *The History of the Evangelical Lutheran Synod and Ministerium of North Carolina.* Philadelphia, 1902.

Biddle, Charles. *The Autobiography of Charles Biddle.* Philadelphia, 1883.

Boles, John B. *The Great Revival, 1787–1805: The Origins of the Southern Evangelical Mind.* Lexington, Ky., 1972.

Bonath, Shawn. "Buck Springs: Archeology of an Old South Plantation." Report, Division of Archives and History, 1978.

Boyd, William K. *Some Eighteenth-Century Tracts concerning North Carolina.* Raleigh, 1927.

———, and Krummel, Charles A. "German Tracts concerning the Lutheran Church in North America during the Eighteenth Century." *North Carolina Historical Review* 7 (1930): 79–147, 225–82.

Brawley, James S. *Rowan County: A Brief History.* Raleigh, 1974.

Brooks, E. M. *History of Rocky River Baptist Church.* N.p., 1928.

Brown, Alexander C. *The Dismal Swamp Canal.* Chesapeake, Va., 1967.

Brown, Nelson. *Life of Henry Evans Sought Out by Nelson Brown.* Fayetteville, 1893.

Calhoon, Robert M. "An Agrarian and Evangelical Culture, 1780–1840." Draft in author's possession.

Carraway, Gertrude S. *The Stanly (Stanley) Family and the Historic John Wright Stanly House.* High Point, N.C., 1969.

Cashion, Jerry Clyde. "Cherokee Indian Removal from North Carolina." Report, Division of Archives and History, 1966.

Clark, Walter, ed. *The State Records of North Carolina.* Vol. 22, Laws, 1715–1776. Goldsboro, 1904.

Clifton, James M. "Golden Grains of White: Rice Planting on the Lower Cape Fear." *North Carolina Historical Review,* 50 (1973): 365–93.

Connor, R. D. W. *Canova's Statue of Washington.* Raleigh, 1920.

———. *Race Elements in the White Population of North Carolina.* Raleigh, 1920.

Crittenden, Charles C. *The Commerce of North Carolina, 1763–1789.* New Haven, 1936.

Crow, Jeffrey J. *The Black Experience in Revolutionary North Carolina.* Raleigh, 1977.

Cruickshank, Helen G., ed. *John and William Bartram's America.* New York, 1957.

Daniels, Jonathan. "North Carolina." *Holiday,* October 1947.

Davis, Edward Hill. *Historical Sketches of Franklin County.* Raleigh, 1948.

Dickins, Samuel. "To the Electors of the District Composed of the Counties of Wake, Orange, and Person" [broadside]. Raleigh, 1816.

Dill, Alonzo T., Jr. "Eighteenth Century New Bern, A History of the Town and Craven County, 1700–1800." *North Carolina Historical Review* 22 (1945): 1–21, 152–75, 293–319, 460–89; 23 (1946): 47–78, 142–71, 325–59, 495–535.

Dunn, Charles W. "A North Carolina Gaelic Bard." *North Carolina Historical Review* 36 (1959): 473–75.

Durrill, Wayne K. "Origins of a Kinship Structure in a Slave Community: The Blacks of Somerset Place, 1786–1862." Report, Division of Archives and History, 1980.

Finlay, Hugh. *Journal Kept by Hugh Finlay, 1773–74.* Brooklyn, 1867.

Foote, William Henry. *Sketches of North Carolina, Historical and Biographical.* New York, 1846.

Fries, Adelaide L., et al., eds. *Records of the Moravians in North Carolina.* 11 vols. Raleigh, 1922–69.

Gadski, Mary Ellen. "The History of the New Bern Academy." Report, New Bern Academy Historical Commission, 1977.

Gehrke, William H. "The Transition from the German to the English Language in North Carolina." *North Carolina Historical Review* 12 (1935):1–19.

Genovese, Eugene D. *Roll, Jordan, Roll: The World the Slaves Made.* New York, 1974.

Gowans, Alan. *Images of American Living: Four Centuries of Architecture and Furniture as Cultural Expression.* Philadelphia, 1964.

Griffin, Frances, ed. *The Three Forks of Muddy Creek.* Winston-Salem, 1974.

Grissom, W. L. *History of Methodism in North Carolina.* Nashville and Dallas, 1905.

Hammer, Carl., Jr. *Rhinelanders on the Yadkin.* Salisbury, N.C., 1965.

Harper, Margaret E. *Fort Defiance and the General.* Hickory, N.C., 1976.

Haworth, Blair. *Museum of Old Domestic Life: Springfield Friends Meeting.* High Point, N.C., 1976.

Hazard, Ebenezer. "The Journal of Ebenezer Hazard in North Carolina, 1777 and 1778." Edited by Hugh B. Johnston. *North Carolina Historical Review* 36 (1959): 358–81.

Henderson, Archibald. "The Creative Forces in Westward Expansion." *North Carolina Booklet* 14, no. 3 (1915): 111–33.

Higginbotham, Don, ed. *The Papers of James Iredell.* 2 vols. Raleigh, 1976.

High Point Historical Society. *John Haley Family History.* High Point, N.C., 1973.

Hill, Michael R. "Historical Research Report: The Person Place of Louisburg, North Carolina." Report, Division of Archives and History, 1980.

"Historic and Architectural Resources of the Tar-Neuse River Basin." Report, Division of Archives and History, 1977.

Holder, Edward M. "Social Life of the Early Moravians in North Carolina." *North Carolina Historical Review* 11 (1934): 167–84.

Hooper, William. "An Address Delivered before the North-Carolina Bible Society, December 1819. . . ." Fayetteville, 1820.

Hoyt, William Henry, ed. *The Papers of Archibald D. Murphey.* 2 vols. Raleigh, 1914.

Hudson, Charles. *The Southeastern Indians.* Knoxville, 1976.

Hunter, Robert, Jr. *Quebec to Carolina in 1785–1786, Being the Travel Diary and Observations of Robert Hunter, Jr., A Young Merchant of London.* Edited by Louis B. Wright and Marion Tinling. San Marino, Calif., 1943.

Iobst, Richard. "A Personal History of David Stone." Report, Division of Archives and History, n.d.

Janson, Charles W. *The Stranger in America, 1793–1806.* London, 1807. Reprint, edited by Carl S. Driver. New York, 1935.

Jefferson, Thomas. *Notes on the State of Virginia.* Edited by William Peden. Chapel Hill, 1954.

Johnson, Guion Griffis. *Ante-Bellum North Carolina: A Social History.* Chapel Hill, 1937.

Johnston, Francis B., and Waterman, Thomas T. *The Early Architecture of North Carolina: A Pictorial Survey.* Chapel Hill, 1941.

Kay, Marvin L. Michael, and Cary, Lorin Lee. "A Demographic Analysis of Colonial North Carolina with Special Emphasis on Slave and Black Populations." A paper presented at History of Blacks in North Carolina and the South Symposium, North Carolina Division of Archives and History, Raleigh, February 1981.

Keith, Alice Barnwell, and Masterson, William H., eds. *The John Gray Blount Papers.* 3 vols. Raleigh, 1952–65.

Lee, Jesse. *Memoir of the Reverend Jesse Lee with Extracts from His Journal.* Edited by Minton Thrift. New York, 1823.

Lefler, Hugh T., and Newsome, Albert R. *North Carolina: The History of a Southern State.* 3d ed. Chapel Hill, 1973.

Lefler, Hugh T., and Powell, William S. *Colonial North Carolina: A History.* New York, 1973.

Lemmon, Sarah McCulloh, ed. *The Pettigrew Papers.* Vol. 1, 1685–1818. Raleigh, 1971.

Lewis, T. M. N., and Kneberg, Madeline. "Oconaluftee Indian Village: An Interpretation of a Cherokee Community of 1750." Report, Cherokee Historical Association, Inc., 1954.

McDonald, Forrest, and McDonald, Ellen Shapiro. "The Ethnic Origins of the American People." *William and Mary Quarterly* (April 1980): 179–99.

McMurray, Helen Johnson. "Historic Mount Pleasant Methodist Episcopal Church in Tanglewood Park." 1974. Methodist Church Papers, Historical Sketches, Duke University Manuscript Department.

McRee, Griffith J., ed. *The Life and Correspondence of James Iredell.* 2 vols. New York, 1857.

Massengill, Stephen E. "The House in the Horseshoe." Report, Division of Archives and History, 1973.

Mathews, Alice E. *Society in Revolutionary North Carolina.* Raleigh, 1976.

Mathews, Donald G. *Religion in the Old South.* Chicago, 1977.

Medley, Mary L. *History of Anson County, North Carolina, 1750–1976.* Wadesboro, N.C., 1976.

Merrens, Harry R. *Colonial North Carolina in the Eighteenth Century: A Study in Historical Geography.* Chapel Hill, 1964.

Meyer, Duane. *The Highland Scots in North Carolina, 1732–1776.* Chapel Hill, 1957.

Miller, Stephen F. *Recollections of New-bern Fifty Years Ago.* Raleigh, 1874.

Miller, William. "Governor's Annual Message, 1816." In *The Journal of the North Carolina House of Commons, 1816*, pp. 3–5.

Morris, Francis G., and Morris, Phyllis M. "Economic Conditions in North Carolina About 1780." *North Carolina Historical Review* 16 (1939): 107–33, 296–327.

Morse, Jedidiah. *The American Geography*. 1789. Reprint. New York, 1970.

Newsome, Albert R., ed. "Twelve North Carolina Counties in 1810–1811." *North Carolina Historical Review* 5 (1928): 413–46; 6 (1929): 67–99, 171–89, 281–309.

Parramore, Thomas C. *Cradle of the Colony: The History of Chowan County and Edenton, North Carolina*. Edenton, 1967.

———, "A Year in Hertford County with Elkanah Watson." *North Carolina Historical Review* 41 (1964): 448–63.

Paths Toward Freedom: A Biographical History of Blacks and Indians in North Carolina by Blacks and Indians. Raleigh, 1976.

Perdue, Theda. *Slavery and Evolution of Cherokee Society*. Knoxville, 1979.

Powell, William S. *When the Past Refused to Die: A History of Caswell County, North Carolina, 1777–1977*. Durham, 1977.

———, ed. *Ye Countrie of Albemarle in Carolina: A Collection of Documents, 1664–1675*. Raleigh, 1958.

Rippy, J. Fred, ed. "A View of the Carolinas in 1783" [Extracts from Francisco de Miranda's diary]. *North Carolina Historical Review* 6 (1929): 362–70.

Robinson, Blackwell P. *A History of Moore County, North Carolina, 1747–1847*. Southern Pines, N.C., 1956.

Saunders, William L., ed. *The Colonial Records of North Carolina*. Vols. 9 (1771–75) and 10 (1775–76). Raleigh, 1890.

Schaw, Janet. *Journal of a Lady of Quality*. Edited by Evangeline W. and Charles McLean Andrews. New Haven, 1921.

Schöpf, Johann David. *Travels in the Confederation*. 2 vols. Translated and edited by Alfred J. Morrison. New York, 1968.

Smith, Daniel Blake. *Inside the Great House: Planter Family Life in Eighteenth-Century Chesapeake Society*. Ithaca, N.Y., 1980.

Smyth, John F. D. *A Tour in the United States of America*. 2 vols. Dublin, 1784.

Person's Ordinary (1774), Littleton High School grounds, Halifax County. N.C. State Archives. Like many inns this one, too, was a stagecoach stop.

115

Dismal Swamp Canal (Camden and Pasquotank counties), the oldest working artificial waterway in the United States, is now part of the intracoastal waterway system, connecting Albemarle Sound with Chesapeake Bay. The Virginia and North Carolina legislatures authorized the canal in 1787 and 1790 respectively. By 1805 it provided limited navigation. It was gradually enlarged in 1826 and 1899 to its present size.

William Byrd, who proposed a canal for the Dismal Swamp in 1728, called it a "dirty place" while George Washington, member of a company that owned forty thousand acres and built the first canal in the 1790s, called the swamp a "glorious paradise."

Stokes, Durward T., "North Carolina and the Great Revival of 1800." *North Carolina Historical Review* 43 (1966): 401–12.

Swaim, Doug, ed. *Carolina Dwelling.* Raleigh, 1978.

———. "North Carolina Folk Housing." In *Carolina Dwelling.* Raleigh, 1978.

Tarlton, William S. "Somerset Place and its Restoration." Report, N.C. Division of State Parks, 1954.

Taylor, Melanie Johnson. "David Stone: A Political Biography." Master's thesis, East Carolina University, 1968.

Turner, Herbert S. *Church in the Old Fields: Hawfields Presbyterian Church and Community in North Carolina.* Chapel Hill, 1962.

Wall, Bennet H. "Ebenezer Pettigrew: An Economic Study of an Antebellum Planter." Ph.D. dissertation, University of North Carolina at Chapel Hill, 1947.

———. "The Founding of the Pettigrew Plantations." *North Carolina Historical Review* 27 (1950): 395–418.

Walton, Gary M., and Shepherd, James F. *The Economic Rise of Early America.* New York, 1979.

Washington, George. *The Diaries of George Washington, 1748–1799.* 5 vols. Edited by John C. Fitzpatrick. Boston and New York, 1846.

Watson, Elkanah. *Men and Times of the Revolution or Memoirs of Elkanah Watson.* New York, 1856.

Waugh, Elizabeth Culbertson. *North Carolina's Capital, Raleigh.* Raleigh, 1967.

Weeks, Stephen B. *Southern Quakers and Slavery.* Baltimore, 1896.

Western Piedmont Council of Governments. *Historic Sites Inventory: A Survey of Alexander, Burke, Caldwell, and Catawba Counties.* N.p., 1975.

Wheeler, John Hill. *Historical Sketches of North Carolina and Eminent North Carolinians.* Columbus, 1884.

Wilborn, Elizabeth W.; Cathey, Boyd; and Cross, Jerry L. "The Roanoke Valley: A Report on the Historic Halifax State Historic Site." Report, Division of Archives and History, 1974.

Wilson, Edwin M. "The Congressional Career of Nathaniel Macon." In *James Sprunt Historical Publications*, vol. 2. Chapel Hill, 1900.

Winborne, Benjamin B. *Colonial and State History, Hertford County, North Carolina.* Murfreesboro, N.C., 1906.

Winston, Robert W. *Andrew Johnson, Plebeian and Patriot.* New York, 1928.

Woodward, Grace Steele. *The Cherokees.* Norman, Okla., 1963.

Wrenn, Tony P., and Little-Stokes, Ruth. *An Inventory of Historic Architecture, Caswell County, North Carolina.* Raleigh, 1979.

Manuscript Sources

Manuscript Department, William R. Perkins Library, Duke University, Durham.

George F. Davidson Papers.
James Iredell Papers.
Thomas Lenoir Papers.
Methodist Church Papers, Historical Sketches.
Journals of William Ormond, Jr.

North Carolina State Archives, Raleigh.

Bertie County Records, Minutes of the Court of Pleas and Quarter Sessions.
Chatham County Records, Minutes of the Court of Pleas and Quarter Sessions.
Josiah Collins Papers.
Mecklenburg County Records, Wills.
United States Census Manuscript Returns: 1790, 1800, 1810, 1820.
Governor Benjamin Williams Papers.

Southern Historical Collection, Louis R. Wilson Library, University of North Carolina, Chapel Hill.

Edmund Ruffin Beckwith Papers.
Cameron Family Papers.
William Gaston Papers.
Ernest Haywood Collection.
Major John A. Lillington's Diary.
Jeremiah Norman's Diary, Stephen B. Weeks Papers.
John Steele Papers.

Acknowledgments

The efforts of many persons have gone into this work. The suggestions that resulted from our public appeal for information as well as the knowledge of experts in many areas have enhanced the quality of this book and facilitated its production. Volunteers who led us to privately owned sites and out-of-the-way places have added materially to the gathering and scope of the information in this volume. To all these contributors the staff is sincerely grateful. We especially wish to thank Catherine Bishir, Jean Boggs, Mary Boyer, Gerald Brooks, Jeffrey Crow, Allen DeHart, Thelma Dempsey, Margaret DeRosset, Gayle Fripp, Ellen Frontis, L. Garibaldi, Jay Gaynor, E. Franklin Grill, Richard Hunter, Mary Hinton Kerr, Sal Levi, Ceci Long, Bettie McKinne, Susan W. Marks, Jesse R. Lankford, Jr., Sylvia Nash, Marge Parker, Lillian Robinson, Theresa Shipp, Elizabeth Smith, Michael Smith, George Stevenson, Jr., Barbara E. Taylor, Gwynne Taylor, John E. Tyler, Margaret Wall, John Woodard, and Ann Wortham.

The staffs of various institutions have also aided our research: the Manuscript Department of the William R. Perkins Library, Duke University; the North Carolina Collection and the Southern Historical Collection of the Louis R. Wilson Library, University of North Carolina at Chapel Hill; and the Archeology and Historic Preservation, Archives and Records, Historic Sites, Iconographic Records, Historical Publications, and Technical Services areas of the Division of Archives and History, North Carolina Department of Cultural Resources. To all of them it is a pleasure to acknowledge our indebtedness and thanks.

Drawings not otherwise credited are from the following sources:

Ashe, Samuel A. *A Biographical History of North Carolina*, 8 vols. Greensboro, 1905–17.

Billings, E. R. *Tobacco: Its History, Varieties, Culture, Manufacture, and Commerce*. Hartford, 1875.

Bogart, Ernest L. *The Economic History of the United States*. New York, 1907.

Butterworth, Benjamin. *The Growth of Industrial Arts*. Washington, D.C., 1892.

Cirker, Blanche, ed. *1800 Woodcuts by Thomas Bewick and His School*. New York, 1962.

Harper's Magazine 19 (November 1859):724

"Skitt" (Taliaferro, Harden E.). *Fisher's (North Carolina) River Scenes and Characters*. New York, 1859.

1 Graham County
Joyce Kilmer Memorial Forest, *Nantahala National Forest.*

Swain County
Oconaluftee Indian Village, *Cherokee.*

Buncombe County
Zebulon B. Vance Birthplace, *Reems Creek Rd.*

McDowell County
Carson House, *Pleasant Gardens vicinity.*

Caldwell County
Fort Defiance, N.C. #268 east of Patterson.

Catawba County
St. Paul's Lutheran Church, *west of Newton.*

2 Rowan County
Grace Lutheran Church, *three miles north of China Grove.*
Archibald Henderson's Law Office, *Salisbury.*
Zion Lutheran Church, *Mount Pleasant Rd. four miles south of Faith.*

Mecklenburg County
Hezekiah Alexander House, *Mint Museum of History, Charlotte.*
Latta Place, *Beattie's Ford Rd. north of Charlotte.*

Forsyth County
Krause-Butner Potter's House, *Bethabara.*
Miksch Tobacco Shop, *Old Salem, Winston-Salem.*
Mount Pleasant Methodist Church, *Tanglewood Park.*
Salem Academy Building, *Salem College, Old Salem, Winston-Salem.*

Salem Tavern, *Old Salem, Winston-Salem.*
Single Brothers' House, *Old Salem, Winston-Salem.*
Winkler's Bakery, *Old Salem, Winston-Salem.*

Anson County
Boggan Hammond House, *Wadesboro.*

Guilford County
Guilford Courthouse National Military Park.
John Haley House, *High Point Museum.*
Dolly Madison Memorial (Isley House), *Greensboro Historical Museum.*
Francis McNairy House, *Greensboro Historical Museum.*

Moore County
House in the Horseshoe, *between Carbonton and Carthage.*
Weymouth Woods Sandhills Nature Preserve, *Southern Pines.*

Caswell County
Brown's Store, *Locust Hill.*

Alamance County
Allen House, *Alamance Battleground State Historic Site.*
Cross Roads Presbyterian Church, *N.C. #119 north of Mebane.*

Orange County
Cameron-Nash Law Office, *Hillsborough.*
Old East Building, *University of North Carolina, Chapel Hill.*

3 Durham County
Bennehan House, *Stagville Plantation State Historic Site.*

Wake County
Canova's Statue of George Washington, *State Capitol, Raleigh.*
Andrew Johnson Birthplace, *Mordecai Historic Park, Raleigh.*
North Carolina State Bank Building (State Credit Union), *New Bern Ave., Raleigh.*

Map of Historic Places

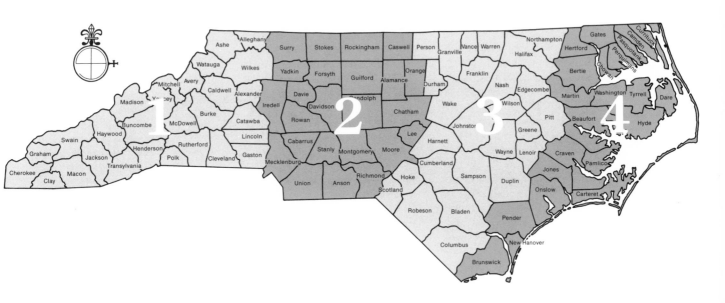

Cumberland County
Nimocks House, *Heritage Square, Fayetteville.*

Vance County
St. John's Episcopal Church, *Williamsboro.*

Edgecombe County
Blount-Bridgers House, *St. Andrew St., Tarboro.*
Pender Museum (Everitt House), *St. Andrew St., Tarboro.*

Warren County
Buck Springs Plantation, *S.R. #1345 four miles north of Vaughan.*

Halifax County
Chockoyotte Aqueduct, *Roanoke Canal, near Weldon.*
Constitution-Burgess House, *Halifax.*
Eagle Tavern, *Halifax.*
Owens House, *Halifax.*
Person's Ordinary, *Littleton High School grounds.*
Sally-Billy House, *Halifax.*

4 Camden County
Dismal Swamp Canal, *Dismal Swamp State Park.*

Hertford County
William Rea Store, *Murfreesboro.*

Chowan County
Barker House, *Edenton.*
County Courthouse, *Edenton.*
Iredell House, *Edenton.*
St. Paul's Episcopal Church, *Edenton.*

Bertie County
Hope Plantation, *N.C. #308 west of Windsor.*
Samuel Cox House, Hope Plantation, *N.C. #308 west of Windsor.*

Washington County
Pettigrew State Park, *near Creswell.*
Somerset Plantation, *near Creswell.*

Beaufort County
County Courthouse, *Washington.*

Craven County
William Gaston's Law Office, *adjoining City Hall, New Bern.*
Masonic Hall and Theater, *Hancock and Johnson Sts., New Bern.*
New Bern Academy, *New and Hancock Sts., New Bern.*
John Wright Stanly House, *New St., New Bern.*
Stevenson House, *Tryon Palace Restoration Complex, New Bern.*
Tryon Palace, *New Bern.*
First Presbyterian Church, *New St., New Bern.*

Pender County
Moore's Creek National Military Park.

New Hanover County
Burgwin-Wright House, *Wilmington.*

Index